AF116747

The Mechanical Boy

An Aviation Enthusiast at Henry Ford's Wayside Inn Boys School

Diana Bittern

Copyright 2024 by Diana Bittern. All rights reserved. No portion of this work may be reproduced without specific written permission from the publisher, except for short excerpts to be used in reviews or promotions.

First Edition

Cover Design: Tory Moore

Book Design: Michael Gursky

ISBN: 979-8-218-50201-0

E-ISBN: 979-8-218-50246-1

The author gratefully acknowledges the support of the Wayside Inn.

Author's Note: All quoted material from the Wayside Inn Boys School student journals and hostess diaries is presented as it appears in the original sources. Any errors or unusual spellings have been retained to preserve the authenticity of the original documents.

Dedicated to my father, Joseph Edward Bittern (né Ochedowski), and in tribute to Henry Ford and the teachers of the Wayside Inn Boys School

Contents

Introduction	1
Chapter 1: The Roots of a Legacy	5
Chapter 2: Ford's Educational Experiment: The Wayside Inn Boys School	13
Chapter 3: The Teachers	25
Chapter 4: Music and the Arts	35
Chapter 5: Aviation Enthusiast	43
Chapter 6: School Life	57
Chapter 7: The Detroiters	79
Chapter 8: After Ford	87
Epilogue	95
Acknowledgements	99
Bibliography	101
Endnotes	103
Image Credits	107

Introduction

The path to uncovering my father's extraordinary life began with a simple question: What was it like for Joseph Ochedowski to be a student at Henry Ford's Wayside Inn Boys School (WIBS)? What started as a curiosity soon became a deep exploration into his past, leading me through archives, family stories, and personal reflections. Along the way, I unearthed not only the details of my father's life but also the broader significance of Ford's visionary educational experiment. This book weaves together my journey of discovery with the historical legacy that shaped my father's life and the lives of so many other boys.

At the Wayside Inn, it started with Ford's dream of honoring the ingenuity of American ancestors and realizing an experiment in education that imbued his students with a love of learning, ultimately equipping them with the skills and confidence to shape their futures. My father, Joseph Ochedowski, was among the boys fortunate enough to be selected to attend the Wayside Inn Boys School in the late 1920s. Ford's vision was rooted in a belief in hands-on learning; that educational approach resonated deeply with my father, who developed an impatience for traditional academic study and a passion for creating, building, and designing.

Henry Ford's purchase of the Wayside Inn in 1923 marked the beginning of his educational experiment: honoring American ingenuity and instilling a love of learning through hands-on education. Ford believed that students could achieve greater confidence and skill by learning through practice. The education my father received ignited a curiosity and determination that traditional academics never could.

Ford's emphasis on hands-on education was driven by his belief that practical experience held greater value than traditional academic learning. Having left school early to work on his family farm and later apprenticing as a machinist, Ford likely developed his 'learn by doing' philosophy as a result of his own journey, which was shaped more by real-world problem-solving than formal education. Whether his personal academic experience played a role, the methods he championed reflected a commitment to teaching skills that he believed would best equip students for life.

I would be remiss not to mention that Henry Ford, despite his contributions to education and industry, espoused troubling views in his life, including the promotion of anti-Semitic rhetoric. These aspects of his legacy stand in stark contrast to the values of education and opportunity he provided at institutions like the Wayside Inn Boys School. My focus remains on the extraordinary opportunities Ford's vision afforded my father and so many other disadvantaged youth, demonstrating that even individuals with deeply flawed beliefs can leave behind a positive and lasting legacy in specific areas of their work.

Chapter 1: The Roots of a Legacy

"A state kid was nothing. We were evil, slaves, or rubbish, thrown out like trash."

Larry Gardner, Wayside Inn Boys School student

In the early 1900s, European immigrants were flocking to the United States. During the peak years of immigration, ports like Baltimore and Ellis Island processed thousands of immigrants daily. Joseph Ochedowski was a second-generation American, a product of two young people who emigrated from Eastern Europe seeking the dream of a new life in America.

Antoni Ochedowski began his journey from Galicia, Poland. He arrived aboard the *SS Kurlander* which sailed from Bremen, Germany, on February 9, 1905, and arrived at the port of Baltimore on February 24. He was 27 years old at the time. That same year, Elżbieta Bąk, a 16-year-old Polish girl from Chocznia, left

Hamburg, Germany, on the steamship *Batavia*, bound for New York. Elzbieta traveled alone. She and Antoni met and after a very short courtship, they were married in February 1912. They settled in Easthampton, MA, but by 1920, they had moved to Holyoke, MA, with their five children.

Joseph, my father and the oldest, was born on November 23, 1912. His siblings Stephanie, Henrietta, Genevieve (Jean), and Mieczyslaw (Fred) were close in age but had little time to establish familial connections with one another. Their lives were uprooted by the tragic and untimely deaths of both their parents. Elzbieta was institutionalized with Encephalitis Lethargica, also known as *sleeping sickness*, a neurological disease that mysteriously swept through the world in the early 20th century. Symptoms could include confusion, hallucinations, psychosis, and personality changes. Joseph remembered only that his mother suffered from some mental illness. She likely experienced significant cognitive or psychiatric impairments affecting her mental state during the period leading to her death in 1925.

Antoni lived on for another five years, afflicted by tuberculosis and finally suffering a cerebral embolism in 1930. However, after his wife's death, he was unable to provide materially for his children, nor was there anyone to look after them during the day. The Massachusetts Department of Public Welfare stepped in and placed the children with foster parents. As Joseph remembered, "On the surface, they seemed decent enough, but they were shortsighted and greedy, occasionally pilfering the small sums of money I was able to earn at odd jobs such as laundry, beating rugs and other errands." It was a lost childhood, with no chance to be a kid, trying to make it on the streets without being exploited or forced into a gang.

Joseph had a state-appointed guardian but little day-to-day supervision. He described himself as a street urchin, navigating the rough streets of Chicopee, Massachusetts, isolated, vulnerable, and with no clear path forward. Fortunately, he was bright and resourceful and was treated with kindness by a shopkeeper named Louise McCauley, who supplied him with pocket money and looked after him during those early days. For reasons unknown, he was relocated about seventy miles east to Hopedale, Massachusetts, where he entered the school system, likely under the care of a foster family. At that time, Hopedale was a company town centered around the Draper Corporation, a major manufacturer of looms for the booming textile industry. Hopedale is a town with a unique history. In 1842, a utopian community was established there, founded on ideals of temperance, nonviolence, and community welfare—a stark contrast to the harsh environment Joseph had known.

A report from the Massachusetts Department of Public Welfare documented that Joseph graduated from the Hopedale Grammar School as class president and at the head of his class. He was reported to be "of superior mental grade."[1]

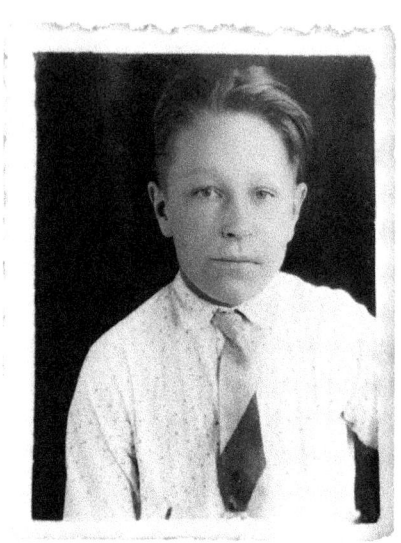

Joseph Ochedowski circa 1925. Bittern family archive.

However, the same report also revealed that "Just before Joseph came to this Department, he suffered an injury to his jaw when his father kicked him. He was treated at the Eye and Ear Infirmary and later at the Massachusetts General Hospital." Further research revealed that the disfigurement to his face was the result of a tumor that was removed, along with several teeth and a section of his upper right jawbone. This information in a medical report was found in his school admittance documents which recorded that, between the ages of 9 and 13, Joseph had undergone seven operations on the right antrum regions, with the right maxilla missing.[2]

Joseph Ochedowski medical record, 1929. Courtesy of The Wayside Inn.

The obvious destruction done by this tumor and repeated surgeries left Joseph with no upper teeth on his right side, difficulty breathing, and what he called a *gangster-like* appearance that affected his self-image throughout his life.

At the same time that Joseph was struggling as a ward of the state, a local newspaper article announced the opening of the Wayside Inn Trade School, reporting that Richard K. Conant, Commissioner of Public Welfare, and his Advisory Board endorsed the plan of sending boys who are state wards, not delinquents, to the school and are "enthusiastically in favor of allowing them to take advantage of the unusual training and educational opportunity."[3]

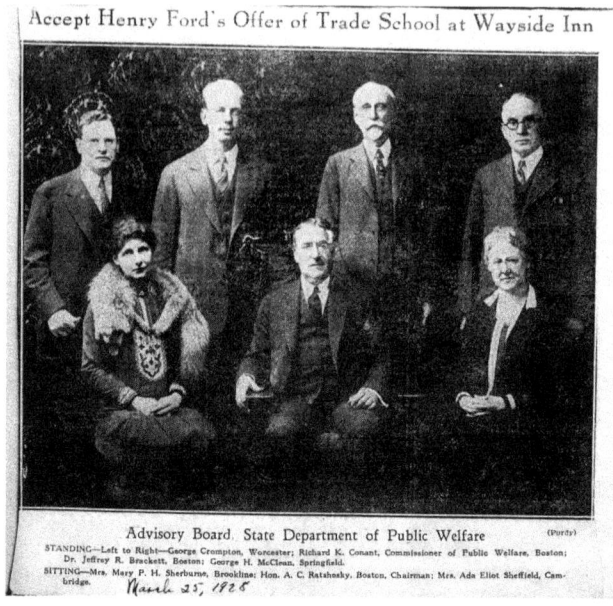

State Department of Public Welfare announcement of the opening of the Wayside Inn Trade School, March 25, 1928. Courtesy of the Sudbury Historical Society.

Joseph's file was brought to the attention of the board, and he was interviewed by Commissioner Richard Conant. Despite his physical handicap, Joseph was subsequently recommended as a candidate after meeting the basic criteria of age, good character, and potential for vocational training. Once selected, he underwent further assessments of his health, aptitude for hands-on learning, and interest in trades that aligned with the school's mission. Given Ford's personal investment in the school, it is likely that he was kept informed about the selection process, making Joseph one of the fortunate beneficiaries.

As an orphan and ward of the state, he matched the demographic Ford aimed to reshape with the Wayside Inn Boys School and was accepted into the school's second class on March 17, 1929. For Joseph, with few prospects beyond the grim realities of poverty and menial labor, the school represented more than an education—it was the difference between a life defined by hardship and one shaped by opportunity.

Chapter 2: Ford's Educational Experiment: The Wayside Inn Boys School

> *They may have been orphans with scarcely a chance in the world, but at Wayside Boys' School the door of opportunity swings wide open to those who would avail themselves of the chance.*
>
> Anonymous, The Sunday *Telegram,* Worcester, MA, October 11, 1931

As Joseph was on the brink of a life-changing experience, the world around him was embracing new freedoms and cultural change. The United States emerged from World War I into a period of unprecedented prosperity. This period was joyful and unrestrained, as if disrupting tradition was expected. Social norms were loosened, especially for women, with new freedoms in fashion, work and personal choices. With their newly gained right to vote, ratified with the Nineteenth Amendment, women celebrated their freedom as wildly outrageous "flappers," with a spirit of rebellion and rejection of traditional values. The jazz movement, born in America during this time, combined the music and rhythms of African culture, blues and ragtime. It became the music of a new generation through its improvisational style and rejection of traditional structure.

Just as jazz represented a cultural shift, the Twenties also ushered in a rise in consumerism and technological innovations like cars, telephones, and radios that transformed daily life. These conveniences gave people new freedoms, even affording them a bit of leisure time.

No one personified this period better than Henry Ford. He rejected the life of farming for which he was destined by family ties. Instead, his rebellious spirit and non-traditional ways of thinking led to a revolution in transportation and reflected the spirit of transformation sweeping across America. Yet, twentieth-century life was evolving so fast that it may have caused Ford to stop and contemplate the direction that modernization was taking the country. He had achieved success beyond his wildest dreams but began to reflect on the lives of his forefathers, who "had better taste and knew more about beauty in the commonplace, everyday things."[4] Unsurprisingly, Ford was vehemently outspoken in his criticism of jazz, linking it with the moral decay associated with smoking, drinking and loose behavior.

In the June 1927 *Atlantic Monthly*, author Jerome Davis wrote about the "significant experiment" Ford was conducting with the education of young people and how he could very well be revolutionizing education as he once revolutionized transportation. His idea was to bridge the gap between the unreality of scholarly education, and the realities of the real world confronting young people. Rather than fighting against a well-established system of public school education, Ford's schools focused on students in the 12-18 year old range, most of whom were unable to take care of themselves. He targeted orphans and wards of the state, who might otherwise never be afforded the opportunity to learn a trade or even attend school.

Ford was heavily influenced by what he saw developing earlier at the Berry School in Rome, Georgia. Established in 1902 by Martha Berry, the school was established to educate local underprivileged boys in vocational, agricultural, and mechanical trades. Seven years later, she opened a school for girls. Henry and his wife Clara became lifelong major benefactors starting in 1921.

Along with Sudbury, Ford began launching schools across the country. In Michigan, he built the Miller School in Dearborn, supporting his philosophy of hands-on learning for young students. In Inkster, he built a high school, to improve the social conditions of the predominantly black population who worked at the Ford Motor Company's Rouge plant. Ford's investment in these schools reflected his belief in the importance of combining vocational training with academic instruction, an approach that would be mirrored in his establishment of the Wayside Inn Boys School.

Perhaps his most notable educational achievements at that time were the Ford Trade Schools built in Dearborn. As a testament to their popularity, the number of people on the permanent waiting list of the Henry Ford Schools—including the Trade School, Apprentice School, Service School—totaled over five thousand.[5]

When the Wayside Inn in Sudbury, Massachusetts, came up for sale in 1923, Ford bought it. He believed that this move would ensure the preservation of a place that was reputedly visited by heroes like George Washington and the Marquis de Lafayette, a place that would honor the spirit of the brave founders of this country. He wrote, "The younger generation knows a good deal about automobiles and airplanes and the radio and movies, but it has nothing to go on when it comes to comprehending the pioneers and what they stood for. There is no use talking about colors to a man who is color-blind."[6]

Ford's work in Sudbury extended beyond the boys' school. Perhaps driven by his passion for preserving historic buildings or by his fondness for the McGuffey Readers—the classic books from which he first learned, including works by Longfellow—he established two additional grade schools for younger students.

The Redstone School was a "little red schoolhouse" that Ford acquired and relocated from nearby Sterling, MA. It is said to be the place where the poem "Mary Had a Little Lamb" was conceived. In this one-room schoolhouse, first through fourth grades were taught. On the other side of the Inn property, he rebuilt the 1849 Southwest School, where grades five through eight were taught.

Redstone School, relocated to the grounds of the Wayside Inn, circa 1930.
Courtesy of The Wayside Inn.

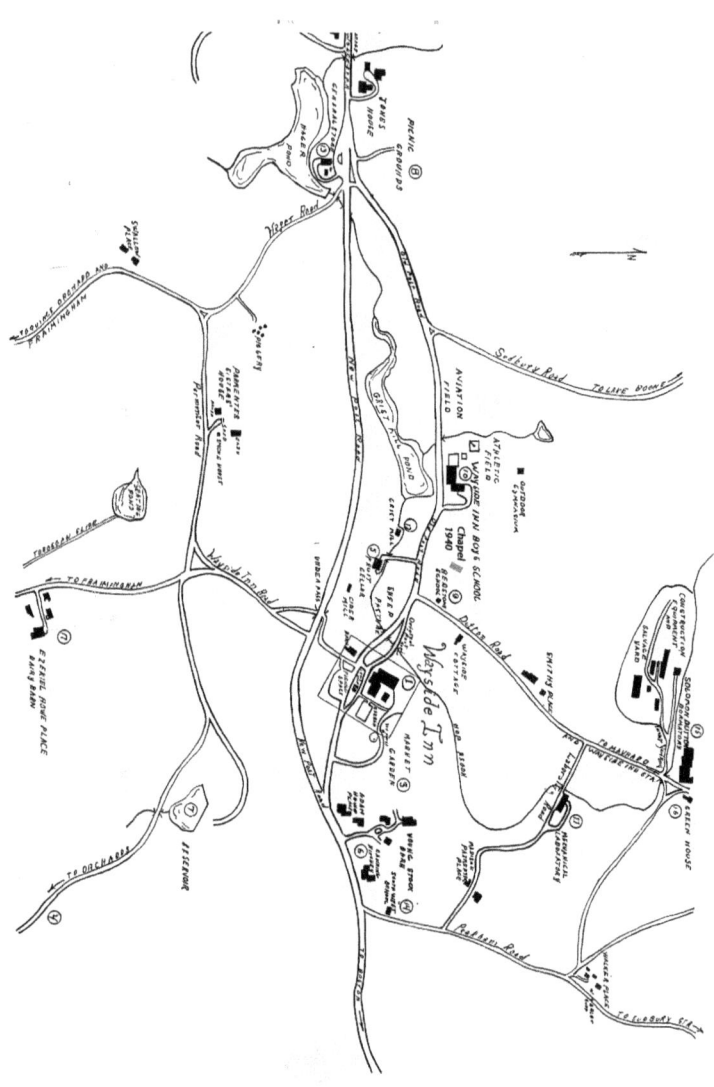

Map of the Wayside Inn, circa 1930. Courtesy of The Wayside Inn.

After Ford bought the Inn, he immediately went to work expanding it, creating a bucolic settlement that would include the Wayside Inn Boys School, which opened four years later in March 1928. In keeping with the resourcefulness and self-reliance of his ancestors, he envisioned the school as a means to promote his learn-by-doing philosophy. A brief article in the November 30, 1927, *New York Times* announced plans to open a school whose curriculum, according to Ford, would include subjects designed to teach boys "how to do things with their hands and how to think." [7]

Ford believed that the lessons of the past could guide the future. He hired innkeepers and hostesses who fostered the same beliefs and love of history as he did. In her April 15, 1930, entry to The Wayside Inn diary, one of the hostesses wrote:

> *The Wayside Inn is not advertised as a place of learning. No professors are called as faculty, no scholars enroll as students in the usual way; and yet the Inn reaches thousands of persons, boys, girls, men, and women each year, and teaches them in a most unusual way. The majority of students, as we will call our guests, are not aware that they are learning. They think that in learning history, for instance, one must read something out of a book, something dull and uninteresting.*
>
> *History, however, and particularly the history of this country, can be learned in a very interesting and practical way – by actually seeing how our forefathers lived.*

Furniture of the 17th and 18th centuries bespeaks the character of the early settlers – simple and sturdy. A bare existence without any of the so-called luxuries of life signifies an earnest desire and struggle for freedom and independence. The very utensils used and painstakingly made by hand have proved to be great steps in the advancement of our economic life. 'History is bunk,' Mr. Ford said. It is bunk, if only read out of a History Book.[8]

THE WAYSIDE INN TRADE SCHOOL – SOUTH SUDBURY, MASS.

The Calvin Howe House became one of the buildings used by the Wayside Inn Boys School. It burned down in 1944. Courtesy of the Sudbury Historical Society.

Ford had several motives for starting the Wayside Inn Boys School. First, he aimed to take advantage of the acreage and facilities of the Wayside Inn farm; second, to take responsibility over teenage boys who, through no fault of their own, had become wards of the state, but were of good character and could pass eighth-grade examinations; and third, to help otherwise disadvantaged young boys become useful members of society—to earn something and learn something.[9]

For the boys lucky enough to be accepted, the Wayside Inn School offered an escape from an otherwise bleak and exploitative existence. In a book called The *Waysiders*, authored by former student Larry Gardner, he recounted his rather grim account of life before being selected to the Boys School, "A state kid was nothing. We were evil, slaves, or rubbish, thrown out like trash."[10] Just as in Joseph's life, it was not unusual that the boys' guardians made handsome profits from money the state wards earned by laboring 60 hours a week when school was not in session. For many of the boys, the Wayside Inn Boys School was the first real home they'd known in their young lives.

Being selected for the School was a lifeline, and it was in this experimental setting that the boys started their new lives. The curriculum combined academic study with practical work maintaining the inn and grounds, for which they were paid a small salary. Reporter Eunice Barnard, who visited the school in 1930, wrote in her article for the *New York Times Magazine,* "In a way, the boys were paid for learning. For his six-and-a-half hour day he receives two dollars, and in the latter years slightly more. Part of this he pays back in board. The rest he budgets for his own clothes, amusements and other expenses. Thus, from the beginning, he is a responsible wage-earner, and, under advice, master of his financial fate, with a bank book of his own."[11]

Instructors were recruited to teach traditional academic subjects as well as craftsmanship and creative ingenuity. The boys developed vocational skills by planting farm crops, working in the grist mill, constructing the chapel under master woodworkers, and helping maintain the Inn.

Ford's educational oversight also included careful monitoring of the boys' health and well-being. Once a month, the resident master gave each boy a physical exam, recording his height and weight, and evaluating academic and vocational progress, and personal traits. The director also advised the students on their budgets and guided them on their personal expenditures.

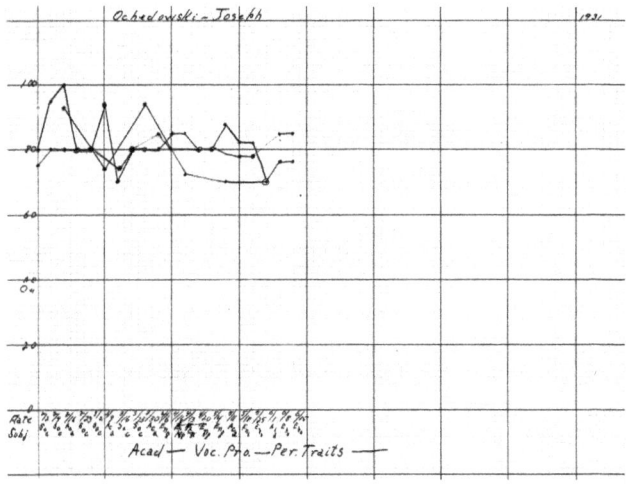

Joseph's 1931 personal growth report. Courtesy of The Wayside Inn.

The students followed a strict diet dictated by Ford's regimen and rooted in his belief that with proper nutrition and exercise, a man should live to be 100. The daily regimen consisted of a breakfast of fruit and milk; and a starchy meal at lunch, including bread made from whole wheat produced in the Inn's grist mill, and complemented with three hot vegetables. Dinner was the protein meal, with meat, vegetables, and soup. There was a strict prohibition on all sweets, except for occasional Sunday ice cream socials. Ford also believed in stimulating digestion with a brisk walk following the evening meal.

In another of Ford's forward-thinking rules, the duty of contributing daily journals was divided among the students and the Inn's hostesses, who also served as music teachers and mentors to the boys. These journals were packaged up every week and mailed to Henry and his wife Clara, who enjoyed reading about school activities, impressions, and, always, the weather. One hundred years later, these student journals and hostess diaries offer historians a detailed, inside look into the day-to-day running of the Inn and Boys School.

As documented in the New York *Times* article, the boy's school curriculum was "startlingly different" from that of a public high or junior high school. There was no language study, except English, and little emphasis on literature. There were no classes in arts or music, the so-called "cultural" subjects, but did include history—mostly about the history of industry, and civics—as it pertained to the rights and privileges of voting citizens. The focus of study was clearly on mathematics and the sciences, as these disciplines formed the foundation for the vocational directions that many students chose to follow.

Ford believed that students learned best when theory followed practice. His project method delayed formal instruction until students encountered a practical problem that required a theoretical solution. In other words, no theoretical teaching was introduced until the necessity of it was required to solve a real-life learning problem.[12]

It would appear that such a curriculum would leave little room for creative expression, but in reality, that was hardly the case. The *Times* author noted, "Out in the fields stands a sizable airplane, built by a boy who hopes one day to fly in it. More and more, it would seem, Mr, Ford is recognizing and aiding such avocations. He has even arranged for music lessons for boys who wish them, and there is a mechanical adviser on duty during the afternoon and evening."[13] My father, in fact, was the boy who built the plane and took advantage of music lessons offered to him.

Chapter 3: The Teachers

> *The only way to really learn is by doing. The trouble with so-called modern education is that it ignores the physical basis of life. We are training children to inhabit a paper world. We teach them to assume that ink is preferable to action.*
>
> Henry Ford, June 1927

In line with the school's focus on practical skills, Ford required that candidates for instructor positions had not only experience teaching basic academics, but also possessed practical expertise in areas essential to running the Inn, such as carpentry, accounting, mechanics, and farming. The Wayside innkeepers and hostesses often doubled as teachers. Local craftspeople and artists were recruited to share their expertise and foster an appreciation of these skills among the students.

One of the most popular teachers who figures prominently in the boys' journals was Mr. [Louis] Varrichione. It is rumored that on one of his road trips, Ford 'discovered' Lou jogging on a road near the school and when he learned of Varrichione's interest in running, he offered him the position of Athletic Director on the spot.[14] While he had no formal education, he was a natural teacher. He functioned as Athletic Director but also acted as a summer camp counselor, role model, and friend to his charges.

Wayside Inn Boys School Faculty 1920. Louis Varrichione is third from left. Courtesy of The Wayside Inn.

Mr. Varrichione was once a professional boxer and became an accomplished football coach. The Boys School football team, under the leadership of Mr. Varrichione and former Naval Academy graduate Stuart Barnett, had a surprising advantage when matched with some of the 'elite' New England schools like Middlesex and Weston High. It is said that some of these schools tried to avoid being on the schedule, fearing humiliation from the *rag-tag* Wayside Boys School team which, despite having little time for practice, was adept at executing a variety of trick plays and pulling off upset victories against their opponents.

To grasp the caliber of instructors Ford attracted to the school, it's important to recognize that they went beyond traditional teaching roles; they often served as parental figures and mentors to the boys. During the summer months, some of the students dispersed to whatever families they had. For those whose only home was the school, the teachers invested time with the boys, offering them new experiences and challenges. These experiences included overnight trips, rugged hikes in the mountains, camping excursions, and visits to New England beaches. Joseph recounted a story when, on a summer camping trip to New Hampshire, he accepted a dare from Mr. Varrichione to stand on his shoulders. What the photo does not reveal is that this acrobatic feat was performed on the edge of a sheer cliff where Varrichione stood. Joseph said, "I was never so scared in my life."

This story is but one example of how the teachers pushed the boys out of their comfort zone, and how they responded to the challenges. In this photo, there is a sense that for Joseph, nothing stood in the way of achieving new heights, including his dream of aviation. One could say that standing on the shoulders of his trusted mentor instilled in him a fortitude and resolve to fly.

Joseph on the shoulders of Louis Varrichione, 1929. Bittern family archive.

While Mr. Varrichione's mentorship helped develop Joseph's character, another instructor, Miss [Anne] Dickerson, introduced him to the piano, fostering a connection that became a source of personal expression. The boys' journals and hostess diaries often mentioned musical performances that included Joe Ochedowski's playing selections on the piano at concerts or to entertain special guests who visited the Wayside Inn.

As one of Anne Dickerson's students, her influence and tutelage were largely responsible for his lifelong passion for the piano.* Like many other Wayside Inn staff, Miss Dickerson was a hostess as well as a piano teacher. Her protective nature was evident in how she wrote about her work, reflecting her care for the boys' well-being. In her hostess diary entry dated March 13, 1931, she expressed her thoughts about the rewards—and challenges—of hostessing. Her words poignantly address the often-ignorant assumptions made by visitors about the boys' school:

> *Queer ideas and fantastic notions take possession of some people; knowing this, we were not surprised unduly when a woman asked today if the children who were dancing... were "all from the orphanage." She seemed quite surprised to learn that Mr. Ford does NOT run an orphan asylum!*
>
> *It is most interesting to note the celerity with which the human mind hops from one conclusion to another, with scarcely a pause between for coherent speech or thought.*

---

* Upon his graduation, Anne Dickerson presented Joseph with a biography of Frédéric Chopin. Inside the front cover, she inscribed, "To Joe, in remembrance of the happiness it has given me to teach him."

We feel it very nearly as much as tho someone had misunderstood us personally when we hear some of the erroneous beliefs uttered by unthinking visitors. Contrasted with such, however, are the perfectly charming and altogether delightful people, who, we are happy to say, make up the majority of our guests – and who intelligently comment on one thing or another in a quiet, capable manner. Many times, unconscious of the fact, they nevertheless frequently impart as much information to the hostess as can be gleaned from hours of reading. It is this class which adds to the job of hostess work and makes us happy in our connection with the old Tavern.[15]

The 1931 Wayside Inn Schools Annual Report announced adoption of the Dalton Plan, which allowed the students to progress as quickly as their abilities allowed.[16] The Dalton Plan, developed in the early 1920s by educator Helen Parkhurst, was influenced by progressive educators like John Dewey. The idea was to foster independence by allowing students to tackle tasks at their own pace and in their own way. The plan also emphasized personal responsibility, intellectual growth, and character development, encouraging students to learn through experience, collaboration, and problem-solving. This plan seemed a perfect fit for the educational methodology already in place in the Wayside Inn Boys School.

The Annual Report also announced that the Boys School had inaugurated a program where the Senior students selected a specific field as their major area of study. The original majors were Restaurant Management, Merchandising, and Social and Physical Sciences, each led by an instructor who also acted as a vocational advisor. Joseph initially chose Social and Physical Sciences as his major but later switched to the newly introduced area of Mechanical Engineering under the guidance of Mr. Howard, an instructor brought in for his expertise in mechanical skills.

Academic study was augmented by vocational training in agriculture, floriculture, mill operation, electricity, plumbing and sheet metal work, woodworking, and automobile repair. Students made frequent field trips to Boston in connection with their studies. Notably, the Wayside Inn also welcomed renowned speakers whose lectures both inspired and influenced the students.

One such visitor to the Inn was Henry Turner Bailey (1865-1931), artist, illustrator, craftsman, teacher, writer, and Dean of the Cleveland School of Art. Shortly before his death, he was invited to lecture the boys at the School. It was the evening of April 27, 1931. Due to a power outage, Bailey addressed the boys in a candlelit ballroom. He spoke about his early days and his education, and how they shaped his beliefs about the place of art in industry and the importance of beauty as well as utility in industrial design.[17]

Deeply influenced by the Arts and Crafts movement, Bailey advocated that art could elevate industrial design, making it not only functional but also aesthetically pleasing. Bailey's contributions played a significant role in shaping modern industrial design. Joseph was deeply influenced by what he heard, as evidenced by the myriad artistic drawings and design sketches he left behind. His letters were often annotated with sketches, and even on napkins and scraps of paper, his imagination was constantly at work creating new and innovative designs.

Ink drawing by Joseph Ochedowski. Bittern family archive.

The diverse talents of the faculty and guest lecturers at the Wayside Inn Boys School offered a singular experience that went far beyond textbooks and traditional classrooms. The boys learned to cultivate skills that shaped both their intellect and character. While each brought their own unique expertise, they collectively helped Ford realize his vision of creating young men who were prepared for the practical demands of life and inspired to pursue their personal passions.

Chapter 4: Music and the Arts

Music is the language of the heart and the soul. It knows no boundaries, and it brings people together in ways that words cannot.

Ignacy Jan Paderewski

Ford's vision of education extended beyond the practical and physical, as he sought to cultivate well-rounded young men. While the school fostered Joseph's developing passion for aviation, it also nurtured another, more intimate side—his love for music. The school's primary focus was technical and vocational training, but the boys were encouraged to explore their creative interests without the constraints of a one-size-fits-all curriculum. For Joseph, this meant the freedom to discover the piano. He began lessons with Mr. Sunbury in 1929, then became a student of Miss Dickerson the following year.

As noted, the school was committed to letting the boys' interests guide their education, recognizing the unique potential in each individual and allowing them to pursue what resonated most deeply within them. While some boys gravitated toward woodworking or agriculture, Joseph balanced his free time between building his plane and the piano.

The boys' journal entry from October 27, 1930, shares the excitement of Joseph's trip to Providence, Rhode Island, to hear celebrated pianist and statesman Ignacy Paderewski* in concert:

> *Joseph Ochedowski left after school hours and went to Providence, Rhode Island to hear Paderewski at Infantry Hall. This is Paderewski's last tour and so it was worth hearing. More of the boys would have gone but they felt as though they were not quite interested enough to go to Providence. Joe loves the piano and is a very good student. He is getting along well as Miss Dickerson is a very good teacher.* [18]

Joseph's trip to Providence marked another defining moment in his young life, where he witnessed artistic genius firsthand at Paderewski's concert. This experience deepened his interest in music and embodied the school's belief that no dream was too big to pursue. Music became Joseph's passion, much like

---

* Ignacy Jan Paderewski (1860-1941) was a world-renowned Polish pianist, whose fame in the early 20th century could be likened to that of a "rock star" in today's terms. In 1930, Paderewski was at the height of his musical career, captivating audiences worldwide with his virtuosic piano performances. His charismatic stage presence and the emotional depth of his playing earned him a massive following, making his concerts highly sought-after events.

his love for flying. The music he created at the piano was not just a pastime; it was a reflection of his inner being, one that the school had helped to unlock.

While music fed Joseph's artistic expression, the school also aimed to cultivate social grace and confidence through another art form. The boys received instruction in ballroom dancing, as part of Ford's objective of giving them a proper appreciation of "gentlemanly" behavior and comportment. Henry and Clara Ford were great enthusiasts of the revival of old-fashioned ballroom dancing. In 1926, they authored a book entitled, *Good Morning*, hailing the dance as one of the oldest and most instinctive forms of human expression. The beautiful, leather-bound book was given to the boys and became their bible for studying the steps, the movements of the body, and comportment on the dance floor.

Joseph's leather-bound copy of *Good Morning*. Bittern family archive.

Ford's notion of dance instruction reached beyond teaching the techniques of movement to addressing issues of 'deportment,' a person's behaviors and manners. According to Ford, "[Dance] is a most effective cure for shyness and self-distrust in public. It is a valuable antidote to awkwardness and hesitancy. It develops self-possession and an easy, competent carriage. And it accomplishes these benefits without expense to natural modesty, for modesty of deportment is one of the prime requirements of the ball room."[19]

One of the teachers, Mr. Benjamin Lovett, was also the dance instructor and a favorite among the boys. He and his wife, listed as "masters of dancing," were instrumental in the creation of the book, responsible for posing the photographs, and arranging the dance descriptions.

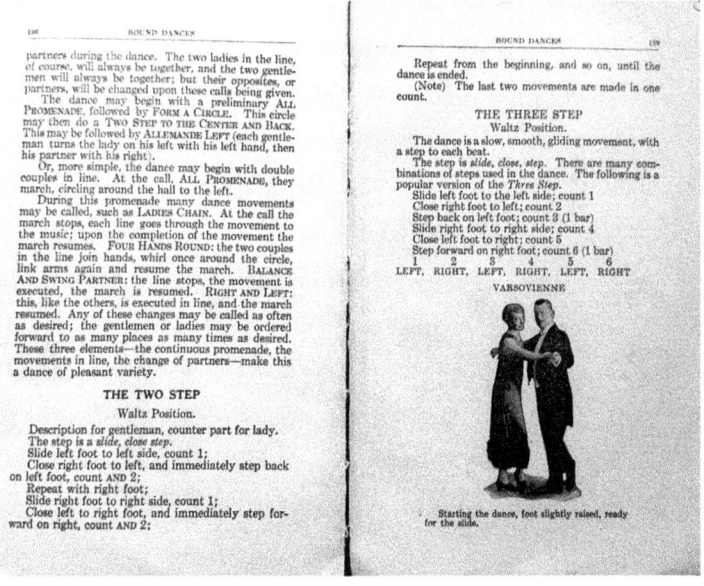

From the Fords' dance instruction book, *Good Morning*. Bittern family archive.

Redstone Schoolhouse elementary students take dance class in the Large Ballroom, circa 1930. Courtesy of The Wayside Inn.

At first, the students viewed dance classes as drudgery, but once girls from surrounding towns were bused in, the lessons didn't seem so bad after all. Friday evenings became the highlight of many students' week, as they guided their partners around the dance floor in the waltz, quadrille, minuet, and schottische. Their instructor, Mr. Lovett, was noted for his two-step and the Virginia Reel. He taught not only the students, but also the staff. The workers, who detested this type of dancing, referred to Friday instruction as the "ballroom follies."

Like his peers, Joseph eagerly anticipated the weekly dance instruction. As a shy boy, he greatly benefited from the instruction in social interaction and the opportunity to engage with his female peers, *as they thought more in "right and left, ladies chain, and promenade...while stepping in with remarkable ease and grace."*[20]

On rare occasions, the boys were honored with visits from Mr. and Mrs. Ford, who actively participated in the dancing. The Fords were like celebrities—bordering on royalty—and the boys were always excited to be in their presence. On June 9, 1930, the boys received a big surprise, as they were invited to attend a formal dance at the Inn. The attire for the boys was dark jackets and white slacks. The boys and their partners marched into the ballroom and were presented to Mr. and Mrs. Ford and their guests. The young dance partners enjoyed an evening of quadrilles, waltzes and heel-and-toe polkas. They were also treated to Mr. and Mrs. Ford dancing the Highland Fling. [21]

Dance Card, July 3, 1930. Student journals. Courtesy of The Wayside Inn.

Through his experiences with music and dance, Joseph discovered his artistic self-expression. While the technical training he received at the Wayside Inn School prepared him for a career in engineering, it was this artistic freedom that allowed him to develop a deeper understanding of beauty, expression, and grace. With such exposure, the school played a pivotal role in shaping Joseph's sensibilities.

Chapter 5: Aviation Enthusiast

> *Science, freedom, beauty, adventure: what more could you ask of life? Aviation combined all the elements I loved.*
>
> Charles Lindbergh, 1930

By the time Joseph entered the Wayside Inn Boys School in the late 1920s, aviation had gripped the world's imagination. It was the Golden Age of Aviation, with airstrips springing up in small towns all over the country. Barnstormers made the circuit, thrilling crowds with their daring acrobatics. People lined up for a chance to fly, and many envisioned a future where there was an airplane in every backyard.

The astonishing success of Charles Lindbergh's transatlantic flight in 1927 turned a little-known barnstormer and air mail pilot into an international icon. *The New York Evening World* called his flight "the greatest feat of a solitary man in the records of the human race."[22] Lindbergh's solo flight across the Atlantic in the *Spirit of St. Louis* also boosted pride in American ingenuity and determination, courage, and a spirit of adventure. It also contributed to a rise in public interest in aviation, inspiring advancements in the aviation industry, increased investment in aircraft development, and expanded commercial aviation.

Technological advancements were making airplanes safer and more reliable, and aviation was seen as the future of transportation. Ford recognized this potential, driving significant investments and innovations in aviation technology. At Ford Motor Company, it began with the development of the Ford Trimotor—the plane in which Joseph first experienced the thrill of flying.

Not surprisingly, Lindbergh's achievement spawned a new generation of young enthusiasts to pursue aviation as a career. At the school, the students were encouraged to start projects in their fields of interest, and the school would sponsor them when they had demonstrated their seriousness and capabilities. The boys' journals and the hostess diaries track Joseph's developing interest in aviation, which led to his decision to build an airplane. One of the earliest clues to the "aviation enthusiast" is chronicled in a diary entry of September 25, 1929:

> *Today at one o'clock, a Ford tri-motor plane entered the Marlboro Air-port. In the evening, most all of the boys and Mr. Varrichione took the trucks and his car to*

go to the airport. Joe Ochedowski and John Lindbergh, the two pilots, decided to go up so they bought their tickets. It was so far into the night that it was dark and they didn't have a chance, for the small plane did not have any lights, 'neither did the airport,' but we all had a grand and glorious time.[23]

1929 Ford Trimotor, "The Tin Goose". Courtesy of the Northwest Airlines History Center.

It was a big event when the Ford Trimotor visited the Marlborough Airport. The Trimotor, known for its robust design and overall reliability, was among the first aircraft used in commercial aviation. It became a symbol of the era's technological advancements and at the time, it was wondrous to behold. The entry from the boys' journal exudes the high level of excitement sparked by the sight of this impressive flying machine. Joseph's schoolmate and fellow "pilot" was John Lindbergh.[*] For Joseph,

---

[*] John Lindbergh was no relation to the aviator, Charles Lindbergh.

observing the plane up close ignited his passion for aviation and sparked his ambition to build an airplane.

Aerial view of the Marlborough Airport, circa 1930. Courtesy of the Marlborough Historical Society.

Finding tangible validation of my father's passion for aviation in the Boys School journals was a revelation. Family events often included tales of how Joseph caught Ford's attention with a small model airplane he had built on his own. However, it was through uncovering photographs and commentary from the Wayside Inn and Ford Archives that the full extent of Joseph's aviation obsession truly came to light.

Joe Ochedowski with his model airplane, Boys School journals, Dec 26, 1929. Courtesy of The Wayside Inn.

By the close of 1929, Joseph's first year at the school, he was well on his way to building an airplane. Joseph recalled the support he received from his school mentors, who facilitated reviews of his design plans by Ford Motor Company's aviation engineers. With each iteration, they made comments and suggestions, and with each revision, the design moved closer to approval. Once it was finally sanctioned, Joseph began construction on his first full-scale airplane.

Skeleton of Joseph's first airplane. Bittern family archive.

As Joseph's excitement grew, the enthusiasm among the other students was infectious. Even the teachers helped by going out of their way to supply materials and parts for the airplane. An entry from the November 4, 1929, student journal documents this event:

> *Mr. Lynch started off early this morning to go to Worcester. He brought back almost all the parts of a motorcycle engine for Joe Ochedowski's airplane. As Joe had been waiting for it for a long time, when at last it arrived, he was very surprised. Now he will work hard in his leisure time to try to assemble it.*[24]

A March 13, 1930, student journal entry read:

Today Joe Ochedowski is all smiles because he received some airplane parts. Joe is coming along fine and he expects to have it running soon.[25]

The first plane, which became known as the *Ochedowski model*, 1930. Bittern family archive.

Joseph's airplane became something of a tourist attraction for visitors to the Inn. On July 17, 1930, the Wayside Inn hosted its Annual County Picnic. Visitors were invited to tour the grounds, enjoy band concerts, and take part in competitive games. Under the Section, General Information is a description of the Wayside Inn Boys School:

> *In March 1928, The Wayside Inn Boys School was established. Thirty boys make this their home while having an academic education as well as learning various trades. The class-room, dormitories, living-room etc. are here. In back of the house are tennis courts, an athletic field – and an airplane – under process of construction by two of the boys.*[26]

49

> Middlesex County Extension Service—Middlesex County Farm Bureau
>
> NINTH
>
> # Annual County Picnic
>
> A
>
> Hearty
>
> # Welcome
>
> Thursday, July 17, 1930   Wayside Inn   South Sudbury, Mass.
>
> ### Program
>
> 9:45 a. m.   Arrival and parking of Automobiles.
> 10:00 a. m.—12 noon Band Concert.
> 10:30 a. m. Horseshoe Tournament—Singles—Championship for Men—Town-Team Championship.
> 11:00 a. m. 4-H Boys' and Girls' Games.
> 12:00 noon Picnic lunch.
> 1:00 p. m.   Band Concert.
> 1:30 p. m.   Speakers:
>   Mr. N. I. Bowditch—Chairman—Pres. County Extension Service.
>   Mr. D. H. Campbell—Welcome—Wayside Inn School for Boys.
>   Mr. Gaspar A. Bacon—President Massachusetts Senate.
>   Mr. A. W. Gilbert—Dept. of Agriculture.
>   Prof. George C. Farley—Mass. Agricultural College.
>   Mr. Walter C. Wardwell—Chairman, County Commissioners.
> 2:00 p. m.—3:30 p. m.   Band Concert.
> 2:15 p. m.   Ball Game—Married Men vs. Single Men.
> 2:15 p. m.   4-H Boys' and Girls' Competitive Sports.
> 3:00 p. m.   Tug-of-War.
>
> ### GENERAL INFORMATION
>
> Autos can be parked at an angle anywhere on the old road from the Country Store to the Wayside Inn School. Cars may be used to drive to the various points of interest. Headquarters will be in the Grove opposite the Country Store at the junction of the new and old State roads. Everyone must register and get a tag for free entrance to all points of interest. Boys from the Wayside Inn School will supply information and direction to all points of interest.

Program from the Wayside Inn County Picnic July 1930, Courtesy of the Sudbury Historical Society.

Visitors were often treated to tours around the grounds or a Sunday dinner cooked by one of the students. On Sunday, May 25, 1930, Miss West, a former housemother, spent the day at the school. As the student journal reported, After *lunch, Miss West and some of the fellows went up to show her Joe's airoplane [sic] and the sheep, goats and cows.*[27]

In 1930, work on the first plane was put aside when Joseph received a Henderson-modified motorcycle engine, recommended for use with the second, more durable plane that was to come. While there is a passing reference about work on the second plane commencing in November 1930, the exact timeline between Joseph's suspending work on his first full-scale plane is not well documented. According to Joseph's recollections, the first airplane was damaged when it was thrown against a tree by a windstorm. However, it appears that the two projects transitioned when the boys received a new design and engine parts. Their excitement, generated by the success of the first full-scale plane, stimulated the boys' interest in taking on a more advanced design requiring more sophisticated skills and resources.

The second plane they built was a Heath Parasol monoplane. This model was originally designed by Edward Heath, who is credited with making airplane construction accessible to anyone with "average mechanical skills" and inspiring the craze of amateur aviation.

The March 1927 *Aero Digest* featured an article introducing the Heath Parasol Sport Plane. Author George McLaughlin announced the production of "a new low-powered monoplane embodying the features appealing to the average flying enthusiast."[28]

THE HEATH PARASOL SPORT PLANE

By George F. McLaughlin

AFTER their extensive experience in building many successful types of light sport planes, the Heath Company is producing a new low-powered monoplane embodying practical features appealing to the average flying enthusiast. The purpose was to produce a sturdy low-cost plane requiring only ordinary skill to fly and maintain. Safety, of course, is given prime consideration and both aerodynamically and structurally the Heath Parasol conforms to approved standards. Due to its inherent stability and light weight the plane should be easily handled by a person with comparatively limited experience and instruction in flying.

Realizing that in order to make a sport plane popular first cost must be really low, the designers have succeeded in simplifying the details to such an extent that the cost has been brought within reach of those who can afford a low priced automobile. The engine used, the Henderson 4-cylinder air cooled vertical type motorcycle engine, is a convenient and economical power plant.

Steel tube is used for the entire fuselage structure, with fittings and wires but no welded joints. Light steel tubes support the engine which is mounted on ash bearers. On either side of the fuselage steel tube struts, with diagonal wire bracing between, support the wing. Inverted V struts above the body support the wing and a 3.3-gallon fuel tank above the cockpit.

The steel tube landing gear is of extremely simple construction, light in weight but rigid and strong. Wheels are 20 by 2 inches, carried on a one inch axle. The tail skid is a flexible steel spring.

Wings are of conventional type, built up with spruce I beams with spruce rib webs and cap strips. The two panels are joined together at the center, with a built-in gravity fuel tank. Tail surfaces are also of conventional structure built up with a light spruce framework.

Any light engine from 20 to 30 h.p. may be used, but as standard equipment the Henderson motorcycle engine has been selected as being the most inexpensive, efficient and reliable. A special propeller conversion has been devised by Heath. For taking off, the engine may be run up so as to develop 23 h.p., but as for normal flight less power is required, the engine may be throttled down when once in the air.

General specifications and performances of the Heath Parasol monoplane: Span, 23 feet; chord, 4 feet 4 inches; wing area, 9½ square feet; angle of incidence, 3 degrees; length overall, 16 feet 9 inches; height overall, 5 feet 10 inches. Weight, empty, 290 pounds; useful load, 225 pounds. Speed range, 32 to 70 m.p.h. Cruising radius, 140 miles.

Powered with a Henderson motorcycle engine, the Heath sport plane presents a real business-like appearance.

From archives of *Aero Digest*, March 1927.

The Heath Company, which went on to popularize *Heath Kits*, electronics kits for young hobbyists, recognized that to popularize a sport plane, cost was a major factor. The designers of the Heath succeeded with a marketing campaign claiming that "cost has been brought within reach of those who can afford a low-priced automobile."* And the Henderson, a 4-cylinder air-cooled vertical engine, was recommended as a "convenient and economical power plant" for the plane.

Aero Digest ad for the Heath Parasol.

The aircraft could be built from a kit or design plans supplied by the Heath Company. It is not clear whether Joseph and his fellow students used the kit or worked from design plans. Regardless of the final cost to the Boys School, or whether they worked from a kit or design plans, Ford recognized the seriousness of Joseph's intent and, through his magnanimous vision, made the resources available to build the plane.

---

* The Heath Parasol monoplane kit, priced at $575 in the late 1920s, was in fact quite a bit more expensive compared to a Ford Model T, which, by 1927, could be purchased for around $260.

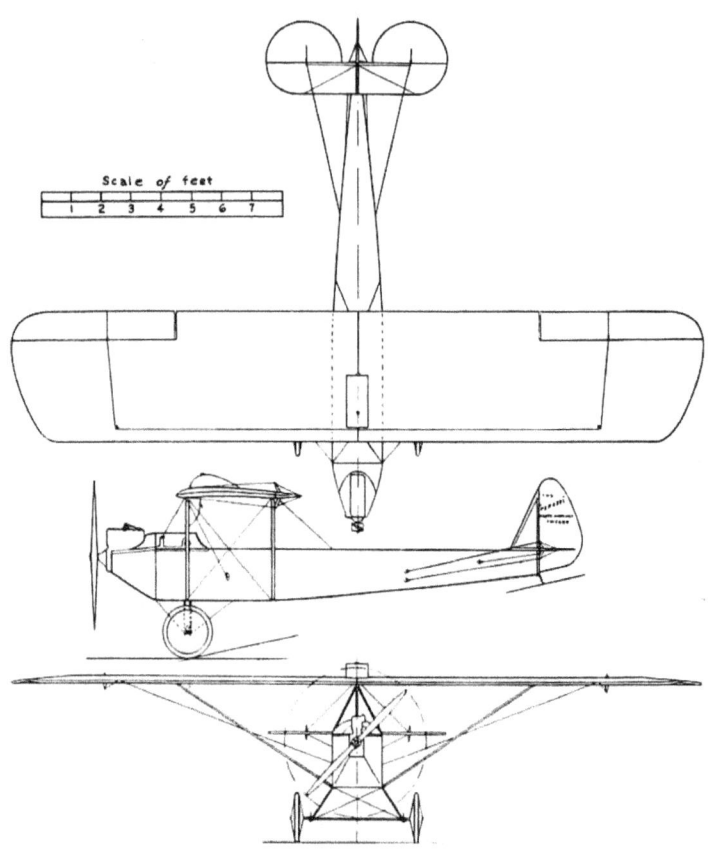

Design specifications for the Heath Parasol Monoplane. *Aero Digest*, 1927.

Wing span	23 ft
Chord	4'4"
Wing area	94 sq. feet
Angle of incidence	3 degrees
Length overall	16' 9"
Weight empty	290 pounds
Recommended load	225 pounds
Speed range	32-70 mph
Cruise radius	140 mile

Heath Parasol Monoplane on display at the New England Air Museum, Windsor Locks, CT. Bittern, 2024.

Chapter 6: School Life

> *The Inn itself is showing thousands of people each year that there is much to be learned from the past, much that can be learned and the knowledge used to make our modern, up-to-date world a better place in which to live. The Wayside Inn Trade School boys have brought a new interest to the Inn; the vigor and confidence of young manhood - and yet they have drawn from the Inn much that has given them a spirit of loyalty and respect for the old.*
>
> Wayside Inn Hostess Diary, January 1, 1930

The boys kept to a routine that adhered to academic instruction in the morning, vocational instruction in the afternoon, and leisure activity in the evening. Here's how one student captured a typical day at the school, noting that for two of the boys, the airplane construction was a noteworthy endeavor:

Today was just another day, as you might say. We went through our regular schedule; that is, got up at 6:00 AM, and worked on the boxing ring until 7:15 AM. We came down and had breakfast, and after breakfast, we made our beds and cleaned up our dormitories. At 8:00 AM, we all had our usual morning assembly. After assembly, we cleaned up the rest of the school and at 8:30 AM the bell rang and called all the boys to their different classes. The boys attended their classes until 11:45 AM and we came home and washed up, changed our clothes, and went for lunch at the Inn at 12:15 PM. After lunch, we came back and read the paper for ten minutes, changed back into our work clothes, and proceeded to work at 1:15 PM.

A group of the boys went into the lab for their classes, that is engineering, plumbing, auto mechanics, electrical, and carpentering. The boys that are agriculturalists went up to the mountain for pruning trees. All these classes were held until 4:30 PM, at which time all classes were concluded for the day as usual. Everybody came back and changed their clothes and washed up for their supper meal at 5:30 PM. After dinner the boys came back to the school and some practiced on their music instruments, others worked on their radios and two of the boys, Joe Ochedowsi and John Lindbergh, worked at constructing an airplane. Two other boys went up to Mr. Borden's home to get some radio parts. The rest of the fellows spent the evening reading books and listening to the radio. The junior boys went to bed at 8:45 PM and at 9:30 the senior boys retired. All lights were out at 9:45 PM and the boys were soon asleep.[29]

The main laboratory inside the Carding Mill, 1930. This floor and the floor below were used by the boys for schoolwork. Courtesy of The Wayside Inn.

In addition to academic and vocational education, the school's philosophy emphasized the importance of teaching dietary health and physical fitness as key components of a well-rounded education. As mentioned earlier, one of the most revered instructors, Mr. Varrichione, saw that the boys remained fit through athletic activities, including track, running, and baseball games. He also led the boys in the construction of a boxing ring.

Joe and Mr. Hatch boxing at Duxbury Beach, MA, July 9, 1930. Courtesy of The Henry Ford.

The students were also given the opportunity to develop leadership and governance skills, which played a role in their personal growth. In his senior year, Joseph was elected as one of the nine squad leaders. Squad leaders were responsible for the appearance and the conduct of the boys in their group. In 1931, a Student Council was formed to represent student issues to the faculty, arbitrate disputes, and communicate the faculty's expectations back to the students. The Council consisted of three seniors and one representative each from the 10th, 9th, and 8th grades. Two of the Student Council members, John Lindbergh and Ralph Delagrieco, were also actively involved in Joseph's aviation project and may have been instrumental in pleading the case for giving the young aviators more time to work on their plane.

While the progress on the airplane was remarkable, Joseph struggled to balance academics with his aviation obsession. His teachers reported that Joseph became preoccupied with the building of his plane to the exclusion of academic tedium. There were numerous comments from his academic reports, as his teachers lamented Joe's preoccupation with his aviation project. In April 1931, Mr. Young wrote, *"[Joe] has already been advised not to be too enthusiastic about the plane to the exclusion of more essential things. Since his endeavor is so sincere, could he be given more time for the plane?"* From Mr. Bushnell, *"A boy who is hard to keep interested unless his work is on a moving machine or highly technical."*[30]

Wayside Inn School for Boys

NAME JOSEPH OCHEDOWSKI SHEET NO. 2

GENERAL MEMO SCHOLARSHIP NO. 54

1931	Department	Instructor	Remarks
Feb 23	Social Science	Mr. Varrichione	Joe is trying very much to do his work well. Is still apt to miss details. His attitude is very good. Has put himself out very much this past week.
Apr. 6	Engineering	Mr. Bushnell	A hard worker who is so anxious to accomplish things that he sacrifices fine workmanship in many places.
Apr. 13	Engineering	Mr. Bushnell	An energetic, enthusiastic worker but one who is not always willing to accept the advise of an older more experienced mind.
Apr. 20	Academics	Mr. Young	He has already been advised not to be too enthusiastic about the plane to the exclusion of more essential things. Since his endeavor is so sincere could he be given more time for plane?
May 4	General Mechanics	Mr. Bushnell	A very ambitious worker when interested but too prone to 'crab' about work which is distasteful to him. Is not willing to take the bitter with the sweet.
May 11	Academics	Mr. Young	Joe has slowed Up. Seems to get peeved easily. I have never noticed it until recently.
June 1	Academics	Mr. Bristol	Joe's thoughts were naturally on his plane this week. In class he seemed more or less elsewhere. As a result he did no better than passing work.
June 8	Engineering	Mr. Bushnell	A boy who is hard to keep interested unless his work is on a moving machine, or highly technical. Joe dislikes to bother with details.

June 17 Graduated

Joseph's Wayside Inn School report, 1931. Courtesy of The Wayside Inn.

During the summer months, there was reduced academic activity at the school. The boys who had no homes to return to were treated to trips to the beach, the mountains, and other local excursions. On July 6, 1930, Joseph and his fellow aviation enthusiasts finally took their first flight when they visited the nearby Marlborough Airport again. Ford maintained that the boys should be responsible for their own money and, with reasonable guidance, they could spend it as they wished. The boys used money from their meager savings to buy tickets for their first flight, and for them, a trip aloft in an airplane was the natural choice:

> *The weather was a little cloudy and there was a storm coming from Bolton towards the airport so the pilot stayed on the ground for a while. When it cleared a little bit, Louis Seligman and Joe Ochedowski asked the pilot if he would fly over the Wayside Inn and the Trade School instead of the usual flight around the city of Marlborough. The pilot said that the storm had changed its course and was heading to go there. So Joe and Louis decided to go over to Marlborough because they were bent on going up. After they had landed, Michael Bolesky and John Lindbergh got into the plane and the pilot told them that the weather had cleared enough so that he could fly over the Wayside Inn. After we were up in the air, we looked down and everything looked so small. The people looked like ants, the houses like toys, and the lakes like mud puddles. At last, we were over the school. Boy! What a sight the school is from the air. Everything was so plain and we could see some of the boys in front of the school waving, so we waved back. After that, we turned around and headed for the airport – satisfied.*[31]

What the young aviators likely saw; aerial view of Wayside Inn and Boys School, circa 1930. Courtesy of The Wayside Inn.

Their first experience flying gave the boys renewed enthusiasm to achieve their goal of building the airplane, and the school fully supported their efforts. When students began at the school, they were given the opportunity to learn about agriculture, mechanical engineering and other vocational subjects. The beauty of the program was that over time, the boys got the chance to specialize in the areas that interested them most. It was Ford's belief that since capability goes hand in hand with interest, there is hardly any distinction.

Joseph and his team were avid in their pursuit of completing work on their plane. On September 23, 1930, the student journalist documented the excitement at the school when their first plane taxied around the aviation field:

> Today, Joseph Ochedowski and John Lindbergh have been working on their airplane and got it just about done. They have been working as much as they could in the little spare time they have and have accomplished very much. The plans have been improving faster and faster so that today at about 2:30 PM, Joe and Mr. Bushnell got the motor started. It was just recess and the classroom boys, including Mr. Bristol ran out to see the long-looked-for sight. Joe got into the plane and taxied around for about ten minutes and then the gas went out. With Mr. Bushnell's assistance, Joe found a lot of mistakes and thereby increase(d) the efficiency of his engine. The engine sounds well and the plane looks very good while taxiing.[32]

Joseph taxiing in the Heath at the Wayside Inn aviation field. Courtesy of The Henry Ford.

Work on the second plane began sometime in November 1930. The boys worked through the winter, using the laboratory in the school basement as their workshop. By the Spring of 1931, the year Joseph would graduate, the Heath was beginning to take shape. Joseph and his team snapped a picture to document their progress.

Joe working on his plane. "It looked like a skeleton glistening in the early morning sun." [33] Courtesy of The Wayside Inn.

Among the new instructors hired during the previous summer was Mr. Howard, who was described as an auto mechanic and an expert airplane mechanic. It is noted that "Joe Ochedowski and John Lindbergh will appreciate this fact because he will be a big help to them in building their airplane."[34]

Two engines with propellers stored in laboratory's basement workshop for cleaning and storage. Left: Heath Parasol; Right: first plane with homemade propeller. Courtesy of The Wayside Inn.

As Joseph's graduation day approached, efforts intensified to complete work on the Heath monoplane. The project became a destination for visitors to the Inn and Boys School, and the excitement was shared by students and faculty alike. On May 31, 1931, one student diarist wrote:

> *Today, several of the younger boys help[ed] the three "aeroplane boys" put the finishing touches on the*

monoplane they are building, by doping, painting etc. In the evening, each of the three boys had the thrill of their lives taxiing around the field in the finished craft.

The progress made is quite remarkable. Following the plans and actually building a plane which not only puts up a good appearance but also is mechanically correct is certainly a worthwhile achievement.

All the boys are very proud of the three boys, and we all give three cheers of Joseph Ochedowski, John Lindbergh, and Ralph Delagrieco.[35]

Joseph with the Heath Parasol Monoplane wing. Bittern family archive.

During the following week on June 3rd, the good news continued:

> *Joseph Ochedowski, John Lindbergh, and Ralph Delagrieco just put the finishing touches on the Heath Parasol plane they have been building. The power is supplied by a Henderson motor. This is a fine new motor and Joseph is very glad to get it.*
>
> *The plane that the three boys are building is the second aeroplane that has been built at the school. This plane was started last November and was to be of sturdy design capable of actual flying. The little plane that was first built gave the boys a good idea of plane construction and from the first plane, many valuable ideas were gained.*
>
> *The boys made most of the wings right here in our own little basement in their spare [time] in the winter. Mr. Bushnell has helped them a great deal in the building of the plane.*
>
> *Since Joseph Ochedowski came here, which is nearly two years ago, he has had a vision of an aeroplane built to fly. This plane was his original idea, and he has directed the building of it.*[36]

Joseph with the Heath monoplane, May 31, 1931. Courtesy of The Henry Ford.

Wayside Inn manager E.J. Boyer reported the following to Frank Campsall, Ford's private secretary, dated June 2, 1931:

> *The airplane that has been in the process of manufacture by Joseph Ochedowski, one of our trade school boys, has been completed and a test flight is to be made tomorrow. This flight will be made by an outside pilot. We shall give you complete information regarding this plane in a special school report.*[37]

The "outside pilot" Boyer referred to would likely have been found at Marlborough Airport. It began as a grass landing strip, first used by barnstorming flyers who flew "by the seat of their pants" using World War I Jennys to ferry passengers when they could get them. The airport itself was opened in 1927 by a Hudson man named Robbins, who built the runway, and the main hangar was built by Francis Kane, a local contractor. The Kane construction business still exists in Marlborough, but the airport has been replaced by an industrial park. However, one student reported that a pilot named Buster Paine was dispatched from the Marlborough Airport to the Wayside Inn School grounds to perform a test flight, but according to the student, the pilot "taxied around but didn't have the nerve to take it into the air."[38]

When Joseph graduated in June 1931, he left behind his airplanes, but his work was not forgotten. At the Boys School, a new academic year was underway. The younger boys took their places as Seniors and continued their studies towards graduation. Joseph's fellow team members, Lindbergh and Delagrieco, continued the aviation project that Joseph started. A fitting tribute to Joseph's vision was described in an October 23, 1931, student journal entry:

> *Delagrieco has worked very fast on the old plane this week, and it will not be long before it is ready to go on exhibition as 'our first plane,' As the covering envelops more and more of the skeleton, it reminds us of those boys, especially Ochedowski, who worked so very diligently in an effort to create a flying machine. We are reminded of the thrill those boys had when the plane just rolled across the field, taxied under its own power, how each boy sat in the wash of the propeller and possibly dreamed of his future in aviation. Is it not fitting then, to repair this weather-beaten relic as a memorial to the pi-*

oneering spirit of those boys who so courageously kept working until we now have, as a result of their efforts, an actual serviceable plane, known as "the Ochedowski Model"?[39]

The Ochedowski Model, October 23, 1931. Courtesy of The Henry Ford.

Joseph understood the privilege he was granted in leading the design and construction of the airplanes, and he took pride in his accomplishments. Yet, later in life, he often mused about the challenges—and disasters—that befell his projects. His first plane was damaged when the wind caught it and threw it against a tree. The second plane, the Heath Parasol monoplane, was destined to become the more airworthy model, but it, too, met an unfortunate fate.

In the days before the FAA, planes were registered with the Aviation Branch of the US Department of Commerce. Aircraft registration numbers, called tail numbers or N-numbers, were issued by the Aeronautics Branch, and N was the classification for US-registered planes. These numbers were often painted on the tail or fuselage of the plane. Records show that the *Heath* was registered in 1931, but little more is known about this plane (or the first plane), after that.

Heath on its nose showing ID number. 1931. Courtesy of The Wayside Inn.

| NC953M | Heath V | S-1 | NC953M | 00.00.31 |

Heath Registration number. From the Civil Aircraft Register.

In the summer of 1932, the *Heath* was stolen from the grounds of the Boys School. Local police reported the plane mysteriously missing on August 17, 1932, surmising that it was partly dismantled and loaded onto a heavy truck and taken away. The police report also noted that a license to operate it had not yet been granted, but tests to the engine were successful, and it was expected that the plane would be licensed.

A newspaper article on the theft appeared in the August 16, *Boston Globe*, noting an unusual detail, "This particular model is banned in this state, and no license could be granted to operate it."*

> **SEARCH FOR PLANE STOLEN AT SUDBURY**
>
> SUDBURY, Aug 16—A low wing monoplane, made by the boys of the Wayside Inn School for Boys, is mysteriously missing. The plane was taken last week, according to Chief of Police S. W. Hall, and a search is being made. Chief Hall said that after an investigation it looks as though the plane was partly dismantled and loaded on a heavy truck.
>
> The plane was built a year ago by boys attending the Ford school here, and was fully equipped and ready for a tryout. Boys at the school said that the wings were beneath the body and for that reason the plane had never been off the ground. The particular model is banned in this State and no license could be granted to operate it.
>
> Tests have been given the engine, however, and it was said that everything worked finely. A large canvas covering had been placed over the plane, and it was expected that it might be possible some time to secure a license to operate the plane. Police say that it was taken in the night time from behind the school.

Report of Plane Stolen from Boys School. The *Boston Globe*, August 16, 1932.

At this point in Joseph's life, regulatory standards for experimental aircraft models were limited. Before the Federal Aviation Administration (FAA) was established, aviation oversight fell to the Aeronautics Branch of the U.S. Department of Commerce, which primarily focused on certifying commercial aircraft and establishing airways. Experimental or homebuilt planes like the Heath Parasol often came under state-level scrutiny, with some states restricting their operation due to inconsistent safety assessments.

Before graduation, Ford received a full report of the 1931 senior class of the Wayside Inn Boys School, including detailed records of the students who would make their way to Detroit. Here is an excerpt from Joseph's report:

---

* There is no evidence of a statewide ban. However, this statement could have stemmed from local safety concerns about homemade planes, as there was no formal certification process in effect before the Federal Aviation Association was established in 1938.

A very serious minded and sensitive boy. Thinks very deeply for a boy of his age and is interested in such subjects as psychology and philosophy. His chief interest is in aviation with music a close second. Practically all of his spare time here at the School has been devoted to airplane construction. He is a tireless worker when interested, but is inclined to sacrifice workmanship for speed. He has an inclination towards day dreaming which should be watched, and is also apt to be a little too serious minded. He seldom smiles which is quite probably traceable to sensitiveness about the loss of his teeth on one side of his mouth. Joe is a really fine boy with wonderful possibilities.

His one ambition at the present time is to get into aviation. This is not a passing fancy. He really means business, as evidenced by the amount of time he has spent in this sort of work.[40]

When Mr. Ford read the report, he took notice and remarked, "I want that boy in Detroit." Ford's private secretary in Dearborn, Michigan was Frank Campsall. Among his many duties was handling all the correspondence, including weekly reports from the Boys School submitted by Earl J. Boyer, Wayside Innkeeper. In his report dated June 19, 1931, Boyer conveyed information about the eight graduating boys, including those who were selected to continue their education in Dearborn. Of Joseph, he wrote:

> *The mechanical boy has already displayed considerable ability. He has constructed two airplanes, the last one is supposed to fly, although it has not yet passed the Federal Inspectors. He has already come to the attention of Mr. Ford and should make the grade there in very good shape.*[41]

There were eight students in the graduating class of 1931.* After Joseph graduated from the Wayside Inn Boys School, he was one of the seven students who accepted the coveted offer to travel to Detroit and continue his training at Ford's trade school. It must have been a bittersweet transition from the supportive, all-encompassing experience of the Boys School. One student's journal captured the mood on the day that the chosen students departed. From the Boys School journal, on July 5th, 1931:

> *Everyone stayed near the house today because the boys were leaving for Detroit in the afternoon and they wanted to be with them these last few hours at the school. The church trips were made as usual in the morning, and again we had a wonderful duck dinner.*
>
> *The "Detroiters" had their bags all packed shortly after dinner and began speaking of writing often, and sending them cards, and all the other formalities that*

---

* The 1931 graduating class included the following: Charles Barkhouse, Michael Bolesky, William Bridges, George Gill, Thomas Margeller, Joseph Ochedowski, Louis Seligman, and Earl Stoddard. Of the eight graduates, Charles Barkhouse remained at the School as an associate instructor; the others traveled to Detroit.

precede a farewell. As the time grew near and the older people arrived to wish the boys good luck and best wishes, a few of them were seen to be holding their lips tightly to hold back their emotions. Mr. Borden, Mr. Boyer, Miss Dickerson, and Miss Ward took the boys to the train in Worcester. The beach wagon carried their bags. Nearly everyone about the Inn went to Worcester or came to the school to say good-bye, and the boys could not disguise their reluctance in going.[42]

Graduating class of 1931. Joseph is at far right. Courtesy of The Wayside Inn.

Chapter 7: The Detroiters

> *We try to stimulate boys to think for themselves by working out practical problems and doing practical work.*
>
> Henry Ford, School of Trades brochure

Henry Ford allowed students to learn at their own pace and in the direction that suited them best. Many of his students graduated into jobs at the Ford plant, but others found careers elsewhere. "No attempt is made to hold them longer than they want to stay, and the founder takes pride in scattering his alumni into different industries."[43]

Although Joseph's time at the Wayside Inn Boys School concluded in 1931, his association with Henry Ford continued for the next ten years in Dearborn, as a student of the Henry Ford

Trade School and then as an employee of the Ford Motor Company.

The Henry Ford School of Trades, established in 1916, educated young men in machining, toolmaking, drafting, and other skilled trades to meet the workforce demands of the Ford Motor Company. It was located in Dearborn, Michigan, next to the Ford Motor Company's Rouge Complex. The Ford Trade School originated the method of cooperative education, whereby the students worked part-time at Ford Motor Company's factories, gaining practical experience and the opportunity to apply what they learned in the classroom to real-world situations.

Because there were no books in print suitable for use in teaching, the instructors created their own lessons, mimeographed copies, and distributed them in class. Over time, each student accumulated a sheaf of papers comprising the equivalent of a full course book.

According to Frederick Searle, Superintendent of the Ford Industrial Schools, "Requests for these sheets were received from other schools in such numbers that we finally bound them in paper covers and sold them to those interested. More than 150,000 copies of previous editions have been furnished to high schools, colleges, industrial and vocational schools, the United States Army and Navy schools, and many individuals in the U.S. and foreign countries."[44] In the short span of one year, Joseph had received the equivalent of a top-notch engineering education that was recognized around the world for its excellence.

One such course, *Shop Theory*, played an important part in the educational program of the Ford Trade School.

Shop Theory, published by McGraw Hill. Courtesy of The Wayside Inn.

Ford's vocational educational philosophy clearly aligned with the requirements of his business. The Ford Trade School and Apprentice School solved the problem of finding competent toolmakers. As the field of mechanical engineering advanced, the demand for skills in fashioning precision tools and dies increased. As a result, these schools saw their enrollment grow from 15 students to as many as 3,500 by the mid-1930s.

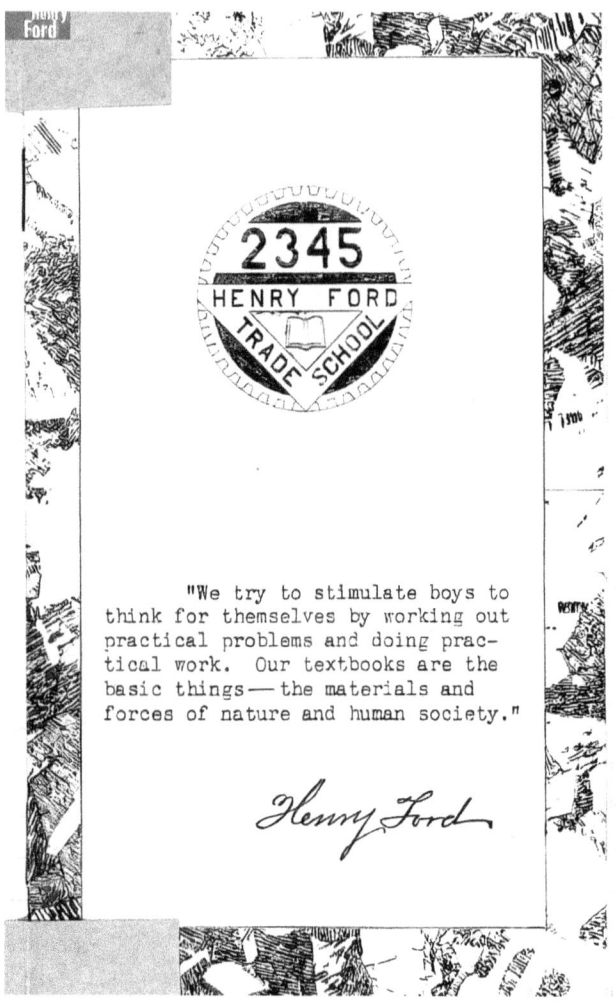

Cover: Henry Ford Trade School Brochure. Courtesy of The Henry Ford.

According to the Ford Motor Company archival records, Joseph spent one year at the Trade School, from July 7, 1931, graduating on June 29, 1932. He began work at the Ford Motor Company the very next day, June 30, at a starting wage of $.50 per hour.

Joseph's graduation from the Boys School and his move to Dearborn coincided with the height of the Great Depression. While the boys at the Wayside Inn School had been relatively insulated from its effects, the Detroiters now faced the harsh realities of the outside world. The automobile industry, including Ford Motor Company, was hit hard by the economic downturn. As demand for automobiles plummeted, many manufacturing plants were forced to reduce production or shut down entirely. This downturn also impacted the Ford Trade School, which saw a decline in enrollment and struggled to remain viable.

Ford implemented a 32-hour work week to distribute employment among more workers, reducing hours while maintaining job security. This strategy kept many employees on the payroll, including those in the cooperative education program at the trade school. In Joseph's case, by October 1932, his hourly wage was reduced to $.37 per hour.[45] And it was during this period, Joseph was laid off. On a whim, he and his friend and former Waysider, John Lindbergh, decided to drive across the country to California. Upon his return, the country was beginning to show signs of recovery, and he was rehired by Ford. As a skilled toolmaker, his pay increased to the impressive rate of $1.00 per hour.

Throughout his time in Detroit, Joseph maintained close ties with many of his compatriots from the Wayside Inn School. The bonds they forged during their time at the school provided a support system as they navigated the challenges of adulthood, particularly during the economic uncertainties of the Depression. Their camaraderie is reflected in family photos that capture their hunting and fishing expeditions and frequent gatherings of the self-proclaimed *Waysiders*. These get-togethers were more than social events; they were reminders of a shared history, even as they moved into different careers.* While their lives pulled them in different directions, his friendships reminded Joseph of his roots and provided a sense of continuity amidst the changes.

Ford's Wayside School Boys at a social gathering in Dearborn, MI, circa 1940. Joseph is second from right. Courtesy of M. Maline.

Joseph continued his study of piano in Detroit under the tutelage of a brilliant teacher named Horace Flinders.† He had dreams

---

* John Lindbergh remained a close friend of Joseph. When he entered the military in 1945, John Lindbergh's draft card listed Joseph Bittern as the "person who will always know your address".
† Horace Flinders, considered a musical genius, was later institutionalized in the Eloise State Hospital in Detroit. Fortunately, there was a doctor named Ira Autschuler who was actively researching music therapy as a treatment. Horace Flinders was one of his success stories.

of breaking into the art world, and Flinders encouraged him to travel to Philadelphia and study with the virtuoso pianist, Joseph Hoffmann. At that time, Hoffmann was Director of the Curtis Institute of Music in Philadelphia, and Flinders was convinced that Joseph, whose emerging artistic talents were prodigious, would be accepted to the school. However, Joseph's pay as a Ford-educated toolmaker was too good to pass up.

Chapter 8: After Ford

> *I am now a full-fledged pilot... I suddenly knew why I had been working so hard for this certificate. All the while I flew, I tried to think of ways to bring about that which I so earnestly desired. In fact, that is the most absorbing ambition that has ever engulfed me.*
>
> Joseph Bittern, September 13, 1945

Interestingly, during his time at the Ford Motor Company, Joseph decided to change his surname to Bittern, not to hide or reject his ethnic origins but to simplify his life. He maintained that the name change was simply a matter of practicality—Ochedowski was often mispronounced, difficult to spell, and was proving cumbersome in the professional world. However, it is possible that his decision had deeper roots. The bittern is a reclusive wading bird in the heron family, and it is also the English translation of his mother's maiden name, Bak. Whether his name choice was consciously made to honor the memory of his mother or was driven purely by simplicity is speculative and something only he knew.

Joseph left the Ford Motor Company for the second time in 1940, got married, and established a successful tool-and-die business called Argo Tool and Engineering Company in Detroit. Although he was unqualified to serve in the military owing to his childhood health issues, his plant was important to the war effort, and he became a successful small business owner. Yet, he found himself unsettled and discontented. A few years later, he severed ties with Detroit, selling the business, divorcing his wife, and relocating back to the East Coast, where he remarried and started building a family home* in rural Simsbury, CT. By the late-40's, Joe was employed at the Hartford Machine Screw Company. By that time, the company had diversified from the manufacture of screws and was producing fuel injection pumps for diesel engines, and parts for the fastener, aircraft, and missile industries.

As shop foreman, Joseph was respected at work, but he felt alienated from his co-workers, who lacked the education and cultural refinement he had acquired during his time at the Boys School. He loved classical music, opera and ballet and had to endure the crude and insensitive remarks of his colleagues. However, he

---

* The house was a design marvel, with unique and ingenious small-space solutions. The most remarkable example is the dining table that is cleverly tucked away on the ceiling. The table can be effortlessly lowered using a sophisticated system of cables and counterweights transforming a practical necessity into a captivating feature.

did join the company's bowling league. Joseph saw bowling as a challenge of physics and engineering. He experimented with altering his bowling ball, ultimately drilling two additional holes. With the control of having all five fingers on the ball, he executed every release with grace and elegance and became one of the consistently high scorers, held in high esteem by his teammates.

When Joe wasn't on the job, renovating the house, raising his family or practicing the piano, he was inventing. One day, he noticed a lawn ornament bird whose wings turned like pinwheels in the wind. "That is NOT how birds fly," he insisted. Using balsa wood, he created a more accurate and realistic lawn bird modeled after Leonardo da Vinci's ornithopter designs in the late 15th Century. He never bothered to patent it; he had proven his point, satisfied his challenge, and it was time to move on to other pursuits.

To augment the family income, Joseph returned to his entrepreneurial roots. He set up a full machine workshop in the basement of our home, where he perfected the design and prototype of a precision gauge indicator holder. He found a distribution channel on Long Island, NY, and began manufacturing indicator holders for the Alina Corporation under the trade name BIRN (BItteRN). The family business became profitable, in part, because it was built on a model of cheap labor. Just as Ford educated his boys in the vocational arts, Joseph trained my brother and me to work the lathe, drill press, and milling machine. We were paid by piecework and learned the value of focused attention and quality output, proud to contribute to the family enterprise and earn spending money in the process.

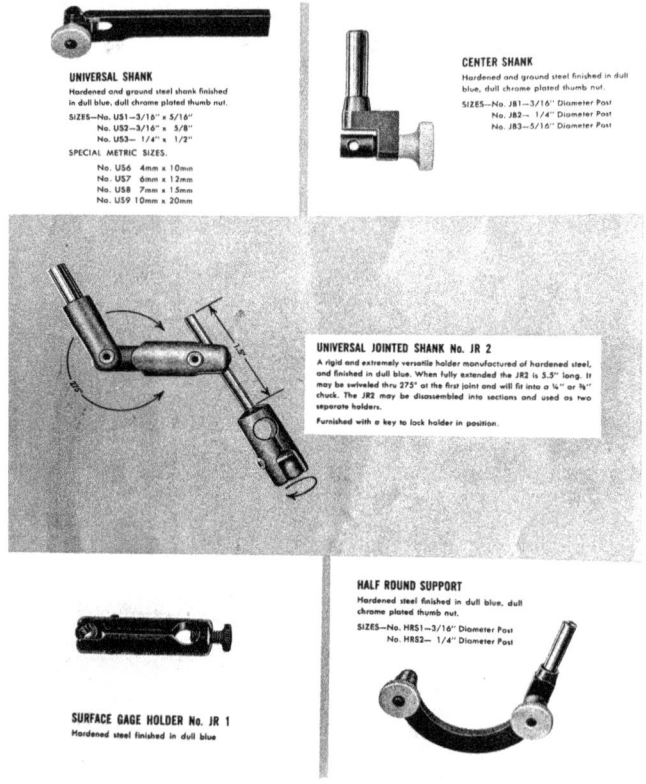

BIRN indicator holders JR1 (bottom left) and JR2 (center) featured in Alina Company brochure. Bittern family archive.

In 1960, Joseph was spending a lot of time at his drafting table, puzzling over a design challenge at work. It involved the complex problem of reshaping the chamber of a fuel pump. One day, there came the exciting news that he had found a solution. Here's how it was entered into Joseph's employee record in 1961:

One of the more difficult parts to manufacture and gauge in the Roosa Master pump is the transfer pump liner. Joe Bittern has now come up with an improved method of manufacture and a method of accurately gauging, which heretofore have defied everyone's best efforts. Joe's contribution has come about through many hours on his own time outside the shop. Joe is to be commended for his effort, and this Incident Report shall become a permanent part of his file.[46]

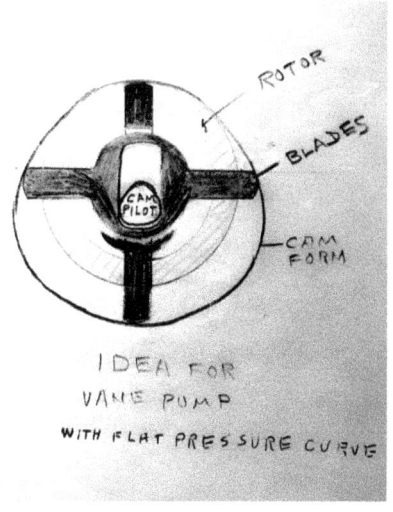

Design for transfer pump liner. Bittern family archive.

Joseph's invention was submitted for a company patent, leading to his promotion to managing engineer. Despite lacking formal education in calculus, Joe demonstrated an extraordinary ability to solve complex differential equations. His Wayside Inn Boys School student records, which noted that "Joe has developed a mechanical ability which is remarkable,"[47] underscored his natural aptitude. But it is also clear how instrumental his mentors were in nurturing his talents, starting with the influence of Mr. Ford himself.

As the company evolved from Standard Screw Company, then Stanadyne, Joseph's talents were again tapped, and his next promotion was to the Capewell Horse Nail Company, acquired by Stanadyne in 1970. In 1903, founder George Capewell commercialized his invention for the efficient manufacture of horseshoe nails, and soon thereafter, Hartford was dubbed the *horseshoe capital of the world*. Joseph's remit was to 'modernize' Capewell's 80-year-old machinery, a challenge he accepted with his usual enthusiasm. Joe spent the remainder of his career at Capewell until his retirement in the early '70s.

Throughout his adult life, Joseph never lost his passion for flying. From his letters written in the mid-40s, Joseph wrote about the excitement of getting his pilot's license, buying a share in a small private plane, and making his first trip from Detroit to Massachusetts to court the woman who became my mother. In a letter he wrote to her on September 17, 1945, this excerpt stands out:

> *"While in the plane, and the lights went out, and the plane was droning through the night, I felt such wonderful peace, such bittersweet oblivion to the rude world that I will never forget it. It was something like, but much deeper than the emotion I felt when I suddenly came from a world of oppression, fear, meanness,*

and frustration to the school at Wayside, where for two years my days were so wondrous free."

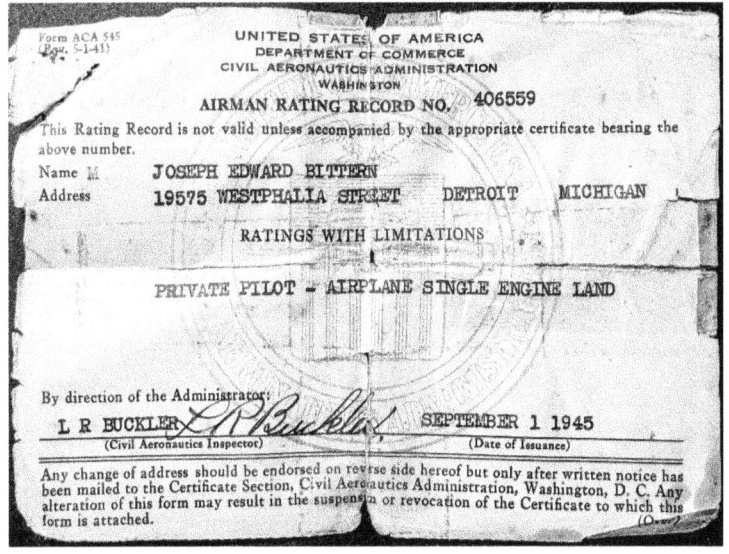

Joseph's pilots license, September 1945. Bittern family archive.

From my earliest recollections, Joseph brought flying into our lives. My earliest memory was when, in a rented airplane, Joseph took off from the Simsbury Airport* and made a short flight over our house. In the late 1950s, I experienced my first commercial flight from Bradley Airport—then called Bradley Field—for a day trip to Washington, DC. My father made sure that the entire experience was infused with the romance of flying—the technical marvel of the aircraft, the elegance of the stewardesses, a

---

* The Simsbury Airport, was established in the mid-1930s, originally as a grass airstrip, for use by local aviation enthusiasts. It remains a regional airport run by the nonprofit Simsbury Airport Association, dedicated to the preservation of this hometown airport.

close-up view of the cockpit, a warm welcome from the pilot, and finally, the exhilarating moment of becoming airborne.

Years later, my father suffered a debilitating stroke, leaving him partially paralyzed and unable to move around without difficulty. Despite his condition, while I was a college student in New York City, he vanished without warning. As we learned only afterward, Joseph had set out to fulfill one last dream. In eight days, he flew around the world, not to see the wonders of the world, but to experience circumnavigating the Earth from the air.

Epilogue

Joseph graduated from the Wayside Inn Boys School a confident and self-aware young man, leaving a notable legacy in the form of his airplanes. His time at the school instilled in him a passion for both the mechanical and the aesthetic. The friendships, guidance, and challenges he experienced during those years were just the beginning of his lifelong pursuit of innovation.

During his time in Detroit, Joseph continued to maintain the balance of artistry and technical skills that had been nurtured at the Wayside Inn Boys School. At Ford's Trade School, his proficiency as a toolmaker was honed, and he gained valuable experience in the evolving field of mechanical engineering. However, his artistic side, fostered through his music studies and his relationship with mentors like Anne Dickerson and Horace Flinders, continued to flourish in parallel. The meticulous craftsmanship required in the technical trades and the creative expression in his music were not in conflict, but rather complementary, each enriching the other. The Wayside Inn School taught him to embrace multiple interests and pursue excellence; whether designing flying machines or playing the piano, Joseph remained rooted in the values he took with him—discipline, creativity and a passion for learning.

Joseph never forgot the opportunities he enjoyed as a student of the Boys School. When he moved back East, he made annual pilgrimages to Sudbury to visit the Inn. The school was long gone, having been destroyed by fire, but his fondness for the place remained etched in his memory.

As Joseph transitioned from his early career at Ford to building a life in Connecticut, his personal curiosity never faded. Whether it was reimagining the mechanics of a bowling ball, tinkering with his ornithopter, or suspending the dining room table on the ceiling to make room for a grand piano, Joseph approached each new challenge with the same determination that had driven him to build his first airplane many years earlier.

His love for aviation which had taken root at the Wayside Inn Boys School never left him. Joseph shared his passion for flying with his children. His career in engineering earned him respect in the professional world, but it was his ability to balance both the technical and the imaginative that defined his legacy. In some ways, Joseph's life was a reflection of Ford's—where practical skill met boundless curiosity. As he circumnavigated the globe late in life, Joseph lived out his dream of flight, a fitting tribute to the man who had spent his entire life pushing the boundaries of what was possible.

Acknowledgements

I am deeply grateful to the many individuals who contributed to the creation of this book.

First, my thanks to Lauren Prescott and Victoria Lento of the Wayside Inn Archive, Lauren Brady and Jim Orr from The Henry Ford in Dearborn, MI; John Gately from Marlborough Historical Society; Francesco Buccella from the Sudbury Historical Society; Ryan Keough from the American Heritage Museum; the dedicated archivists who supported my research and furnished the factual details, bringing the past to life in ways that my words alone could not achieve. My thanks to Professor Michael McCluskey, whose research into the Wayside Inn Boys School and guidance helped me launch this project; his encouragement, insightful editorial suggestions and organizational expertise were invaluable in shaping the narrative. Thanks to acclaimed Wayside Inn historian and author Brian Plumb, who assisted me with editorial and publishing guidance and photo restoration, breathing new life into the images accompanying this story. The visual elements are as crucial as the text and his contributions truly enhance the reader's experience.

To my sister Madeline, and my cousins Mark, Ted, and Jean, for their contributions of stories and photos from family ancestry archives that helped bring this book to fruition. Thank you to my soul sister Valerie Shepherd for her support and spot-on editorial suggestions. And heartfelt thanks to my late brother, Arwin, whose high school interview with our father provided invaluable first-hand details of his early life. These contributions have made this journey not only possible but deeply rewarding.

Finally, to my husband Michael, whose editorial and layout expertise was second only to his heroic tolerance during the book birthing process.

Bibliography

Aero Digest. "The Heath Parasol Sport Plane." Written by George McLaughlin. March 1927.

Barnard, Eunice Fuller. "Henry Ford Invents a School." *New York Times Magazine*, April 13, 1930.

Boston Globe. "Report of Plane Stolen from Boys School." August 16, 1932.

Bryson, Bill. *One Summer: America, 1927*. New York: Anchor Books, 2013.

Chamberlain, Samuel. *Longfellow's Wayside Inn: A Camera Impression*. New York: Hastings House Publishers, 1938.

Davis, Jerome. "Henry Ford, Educator." *Atlantic Monthly*, June 1927, 803-809.

Ford, Henry, and Clara Ford. *Good Morning*. Dearborn, MI: Dearborn Publishing Company, 1926.

Ford, Henry. *My Life and Work*. New York: Garden City Publishing Company, 1927. Courtesy of the Sudbury Historical Society.

Ford, Henry. "Why I Bought the Wayside Inn and What I Am Doing with It." *Garden and Home Builder*, July 1926, 433-434.

Ford Trade School. *Shop Theory*. Revised edition. New York: McGraw-Hill Publishing.

Gardner, Larry. *The Waysiders*. Sudbury, MA: Sudbury Historical Society.

Garfield, Curtis, and Alice Ridley. *Henry Ford's Boys: The Story of the Wayside Inn Boys School*. Sudbury, MA: Porcupine Enterprises, 1998.

Graves, Ralph H. *The Triumph of an Idea: The Story of Henry Ford*. Garden City, NY: Doubleday, Doran, 1934. Accessed from https://catalog.hathitrust.org/Record/001598601.

McCluskey, Dr. Michael. Northeastern University. Tales of a Wayside School. May 2023. https://www.youtube.com/watch?v=-bmPxkh-2co.

New York Times. "Ford School at Sudbury." November 22, 1927.

Parkinson, Helen. *Education on the Dalton Plan*. 1922. Accessed from https://daltoninternational.org/dalton-education/.

Plumb, Brian. *A History of Longfellow's Wayside Inn*. 2011. The History Press, Charleston SC.

Rouge Reporter. "The Wayside Inn Boys School." Written by Linton Wells. 1940.

Sunday Telegram. "Paying Orphans $2 a Day to Go to School." October 11, 1931.

The Henry Ford Archives. Dearborn, Michigan.

Wayside Inn Boys School Diaries. Wayside Inn Archive, Sudbury, MA.

Endnotes

The Roots of a Legacy

1. General Report, Joseph Ochedowski. Box 169: Wayside Inn Boys School Records (Ochedowski to Racznski), The Wayside Inn Collection, The Wayside Inn Foundation.
2. Administrative Record: Joseph Ochedowski. Box 169: Wayside Inn Boys School Records (Ochedowski to Racznski), The Wayside Inn Collection, The Wayside Inn Foundation.
3. Sudbury Advisory Board Accepts Henry Ford's Offer of Trade School at Wayside Inn. (unnamed) March 25, 1928. 2002.004.0009.

Ford's Educational Experiment

4. Henry Ford, "Why I Bought the Wayside Inn and What I am Doing With It," *Garden & Home Builder*, July 1926: p. 433.
5. Jerome Davis, "Henry Ford, Educator", *The Atlantic Monthly*. June 1927, p. 803.
6. Henry Ford, "Why I Bought the Wayside Inn and What I am Doing With It," p.434.
7. "Ford School at Sudbury." *The New York Times*. November 22, 1927.

8. Wayside Inn as a place of learning, April 15, 1930. Box 181. The Wayside Inn Collection, The Wayside Inn Foundation.
9. Linton Wells, "The Wayside Inn Boys School," *Rouge Reporter*. 1940.
10. Larry Gardner, *The Waysiders*. Sudbury Historical Society.
11. Eunice Barnard, "Henry Ford Invents a School," *The New York Times*, April 13, 1930, p. 2.
12. Jerome Davis, "Henry Ford, Educator," *The Atlantic Monthly*, June 1927, p. 805.
13. Eunice Barnard, "Henry Ford Invents a School", p. 2.

The Teachers

14. Curtis F. Garfield and Alison R. Ridley. *Henry Ford's Boys*. Sudbury: Porcupine Enterprises, 1998, p. 157.
15. Ann Dickerson, on visitors. February 27, 1931. Box 181 #1, WIBS Diaries. The Wayside Inn Collection, The Wayside Inn Foundation.
16 From the Collections of The Henry Ford, Accession #111, Box 13. Wayside Inn Boys School Annual Report 1931.
17. From the Collections of The Henry Ford, Accession #111, Boys School Diaries, Box 13, April 27, 1931. Henry Turner Bailey visit.

Music and the Arts

18. From the Collections of The Henry Ford, Accession #111, Box 12, Boys School Diaries, October 27, 1930. Joe travels to attend Paderewski concert in RI.
19. Henry and Clara Ford. *Good Morning*. Dearborn Publishing Company, 1926.
20. From the Collections of The Henry Ford, Accession #111, Box 4, Boys School Diaries, January 10, 1930. Dance instruction.
21. From the Collections of The Henry Ford, Accession #111, Box 12, Boys School Diaries, June 9, 1930. Formal dance with Mr. and Mrs. Ford in attendance.

Aviation Enthusiast

22. Bill Bryson, *One Summer: America, 1927*. Anchor Books. 2013. p.99.
23. From the Collections of The Henry Ford, Accession #111, Boys School Diaries, Box 12, September 25, 1929, student journal entry. Marlboro Airport.
24. From the Collections of The Henry Ford, Accession #111, Boys School Diaries, Box 12, November 4, 1929, student journal entry. Motorcycle parts for the engine.
25. From the Collections of The Henry Ford, Accession #111, Boys School Diaries, Box 12, March 13, 1930, student journal entry. Airplane parts.
26. Wayside Inn County Picnic program, July 17, 1930. Sudbury Historical Society. 2002.005.0049.
27. From the Collections of The Henry Ford, Accession #111, Boys School Diaries, Box 12, May 25, 1930, student journal entry, Miss West views the airplane.
28. George McLaughlin, "The Heath Parasol Sport Plane." *Aero Digest*. March 1927.

School Life

29. From the Collections of The Henry Ford, Accession #111, Boys School Diaries, Box 12, March 25, 1930. A typical day.
30. Joseph Ochedowski, Academic Report, April 1931. The Wayside Inn Collection, The Wayside Inn Foundation.
31. From the Collections of The Henry Ford Accession #111, Boys School Diaries, Box 12, July 6, 1930. Marlborough Airport plane ride.
32. From the Collections of The Henry Ford Accession #111, Boys School Diaries, Box 12, September 23, 1930. Joseph taxis in Heath.
33. From the Collections of The Henry Ford, Accession #111, Boys School Diaries, Box 13, April 27, 1931. Joseph posing with skeleton of plane.
34. From the Collections of The Henry Ford, Accession #111, Boys School Diaries, Box 13, August 27, 1930. Mr. Howard hired.

35. From the Collections of The Henry Ford Accession #111, Boys School Diaries, Box 13, May 31, 1931. Three cheers for the builders.
36. From the Collections of The Henry Ford Accession #111, Boys School Diaries, Box 13, June 3, 1931. Joseph's vision.
37. From the Collections of The Henry Ford, Accession #292, Box 13, Frank Campsall report, June 2, 1931. Plane test flight.
38. Larry Gardner, The Waysiders. Sudbury Historical Society.
39. From the Collections of The Henry Ford, Accession #111, Box 13, Boys School Diaries, October 23, 1931. The Ochedowski model.
40. From the Collections of The Henry Ford, Accession #111, Box 13, June 19, 1931. Graduating report, Joseph Ochedowski.
41. From the Collections of The Henry Ford, Accession #292, Box 14, June 19, 1931. Frank Campsall report, Joseph Ochedowski.
42. The Detroiters, July 5 1931, Box 181. WIBS Diaries. The Wayside Inn Collection, The Wayside Inn Foundation.

The Detroiters

43. Ralph H. Graves, *The Triumph of an Idea,* 1934. Doubleday, Doran, p. 119.
44. Ford Trade School, *Shop Theory,* Revised Edition. McGraw Hill.
45. Ford Motor Company Archives. Employment records for Joseph Ochedowski / Joseph Bittern, June 1932 to June 1940.

After Ford

46. Joseph Bittern employment records, Stanadyne (formerly Hartford Machine Screw Co.), 1961.
47. Boys School Report, Campbell, April 19, 1931. Box 181 #1, WIBS Diaries. The Wayside Inn Collection, The Wayside Inn Foundation.

Image Credits

The Roots of a Legacy

Joseph Edward Ochedowski, circa 1922. Bittern family archive.

Medical Record: Joseph Ochedowski. Box 169, #34. The Wayside Inn Collection, The Wayside Inn Foundation.

Newspaper article, *Advisory Board Accepts Henry Ford's Offer of Trade School at Wayside Inn*. (unnamed) March 25, 1928. Sudbury Historical Society.

Ford's Educational Experiment

Group of students outside Redstone School, 1937. Album 23 #56. The Wayside Inn Collection, The Wayside Inn Foundation.

Wayside inn Ford Era Map 1930 drawn by student. Box 199, #10. The Wayside Inn Collection, The Wayside Inn Foundation.

Calvin Howe House, which became the Wayside Inn Boys School. Sudbury Historical Society, 2014.056.0011.

Progress report for Joseph Ochedowski, 1931. Box 169, #34. The Wayside Inn Collection, The Wayside Inn Foundation.

The Teachers

Faculty members of the Wayside Inn, September 25, 1929. Box 15, #4. The Wayside Inn Collection, The Wayside Inn Foundation.

Joseph on the shoulders of Louis Varrichione, 1929. Bittern family archive.

Ink drawing by Joseph Ochedowski. Bittern family archive.

Music and the Arts

Joseph's leather-bound copy of *Good Morning*. Bittern family archive.

From the Fords' dance instruction book, *Good Morning*. Bittern family archive.

Redstone Schoolhouse elementary students take dance class in the Large Ballroom. The Wayside Inn Collection, The Wayside Inn Foundation.

Dance card, July 3, 1930. Box 180, #4. The Wayside Inn Collection, The Wayside Inn Foundation.

Aviation Enthusiast

1929 Ford Trimotor, "The Tin Goose." Northwest Airlines History Center.

Aerial view of the Marlborough Airport, circa 1930. Marlborough Historical Society.

Joe Ochedowski with his model airplane, Wayside Inn Boys School journals, Dec 26, 1929. Box 15, #4. The Wayside Inn Collection, The Wayside Inn Foundation.

Skeleton of Joseph's first airplane. Bittern family archive.

The first plane, The Ochedowski model, 1930. Bittern family archive.

Wayside Inn County Picnic program, July 17, 1930. Sudbury Historical Society.

Introducing The Heath Parasol Sport Plane, Vol. 10, No. 3, March 1927. Aero Digest.

Advertisement for the Heath Parasol. *Aero Digest*, Vol. 10, No. 3, March 1927, p. 232. Aero Digest.

Design specifications for the Heath Parasol Monoplane. Aero Digest.

Heath Parasol Monoplane on display at the New England Air Museum, Windsor Locks, CT. Bittern family archive.

School Life

The main laboratory inside the Carding Mill, April 9, 1930. Hostess diaries. The Wayside Inn Collection, The Wayside Inn Foundation.

Joe and Mr. Hatch boxing at Duxbury Beach, MA. July 9, 1930. THF719962. The Henry Ford.

Joseph Ochedowski academic remarks, Feb 23, 1931-June 8, 1931. Box 169, #34. The Wayside Inn Collection, The Wayside Inn Foundation.

Aerial view approaching from the southeast. Note carriage house on the north side of Wayside Inn road which places this before 1939 when the carriage house was moved. Album 17, #2. The Wayside Inn Collection, The Wayside Inn Foundation.

Joseph taxiing at the Wayside Inn aviation field. THF720121. The Henry Ford.

Joseph Ochedowski with the aereoplane [sic] he is building, May 15, 1930. Box 180, #3. The Wayside Inn Collection, The Wayside Inn Foundation.

Motors. The two airplane motors set up in the basement for cleaning preparatory to winter storage. The new one is on the left, while that to the right is the old motor with its homemade propellor [sic]. November 29, 1931. Box 181, #2. The Wayside Inn Collection, The Wayside Inn Foundation.

Joseph with the Heath Parasol Monoplane wing. Bittern amily Archive.

Joseph with the Heath monoplane, May 31, 1931. THF720122. The Henry Ford.

The Ochedowski Model, October 23, 1930. THF720124. The Henry Ford.

Heath plane on its nose, showing ID number. The Wayside Inn Collection, The Wayside Inn Foundation.

Heath registration number. From the Civil Aircraft Register. http://www.airhistory.org.uk/gy/reg_N90.html.

Report of plane stolen from Boys School, August 16, 1932. *The Boston Globe.*

Entire senior group, Wayside Inn Boys School journals, June 21, 1931. Box 191, #2. The Wayside Inn Collection, The Wayside Inn Foundation.

The Detroiters

Shop Theory, the Henry Ford Trade School. Published by McGraw Hill, August 1944. The Wayside Inn Collection, The Wayside Inn Foundation.

Cover, Henry Ford Trade School Brochure. THF223507. The Henry Ford.

Ford's Wayside School Boys, Dearborn, MI, circa 1940. M. Maline.

After Ford

BIRN indicator holders. Bittern family archive.

Design for transfer pump liner. Bittern family archive.

Joseph Bittern, private pilot's license, September 1945. Bittern family archive.

About the Author

Diana Bittern is a first-time author, having spent her career in STEM database publishing, specializing in medical and engineering content. Her love of flying, fast cars, and dance, passed down from her father, along with nostalgic and poignant stories from his time at the Wayside Inn Boys School, led her to uncover the extraordinary story behind *The Mechanical Boy*. Her narrative blends personal family history with a broader historical context. Diana is married, has a daughter and stepson, and divides her time between her childhood home in Connecticut and the New York City metro area.

www.ingramcontent.com/pod-product-compliance
Lightning Source LLC
LaVergne TN
LVHW061047070526
838201LV00074B/5210